DATE DUE

APR 1 8 1996			
DEC 3 1996			

Demco, Inc. 38-293

CLEOPATRA

Other books by Polly Schoyer Brooks

BEYOND THE MYTH:
The Story of Joan of Arc

QUEEN ELEANOR:
Independent Spirit of the Medieval World
A biography of Eleanor of Aquitaine

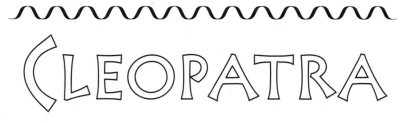

CLEOPATRA

Goddess of Egypt,
Enemy of Rome

- BY -

POLLY SCHOYER BROOKS

HarperCollins*Publishers*

Every effort has been made to locate copyright holders of all copyrighted materials and secure the necessary permission to reproduce them. In the event of any questions arising as to their use, the publisher will be glad to make changes in future printings and editions.

Excerpts on pages 93 and 118 from *The Complete Poems of Cavafy*, copyright © 1961 and renewed 1989 by Rae Dalven, reprinted by permission of Harcourt Brace and Company. Excerpt on page 126 from *The Odes of Horace* by Horace. Translation copyright © 1965 by James Michie. Used by permission of Viking Penguin, a division of Penguin Books USA Inc.

In addition we acknowledge the following individuals and institutions for the illustrations provided to us, and list the pages on which the illustrations appear:

Page 8: A private American collection; pages 8, 17: Allan Mitchell; page 10: British Museum; pages 22–23, 44, 69, 94–95: The Metropolitan Museum of Art; Page 28: Museo Nazionale; pages 36–37: The Bettman Archive; pages 40–41, 65, 74, 87, 104, 122–123: Art Resource; page 52: Antikeusammlung Staatliche Museum zu Berlin Preussischer Kulturbesitz; pages 58–59: The New York Public Library; page 125: The New York Zoological Society.

Map on page viii: Turner Brooks; maps on pages 60 and 108: Pat Tobin.

Library of Congress Cataloging-in-Publication Data
Brooks, Polly Schoyer.
  Cleopatra : goddess of Egypt, enemy of Rome / by Polly Schoyer Brooks.
    p.   cm.
  Includes bibliographical references, index.
  ISBN 0-06-023608-6 (lib. bdg.) — ISBN 0-06-023607-8
  1. Cleopatra, Queen of Egypt, d. 30. B.C.—Juvenile literature.
2. Queens—Egypt—Biography—Juvenile literature.   I. Title.
DT92.7.B77   1995   95-10688
932'.021'092—dc20   CIP
[B]   AC

Typography by Elynn Cohen
1 2 3 4 5 6 7 8 9 10
❖
First Edition

To my lovely Jessica

CONTENTS

Introduction: Cleopatra's World — 1

1. Cleopatra Grows Up — 5
2. Cleopatra's Visit to the Nile — 19
3. Cleopatra Meets Caesar — 26
4. Caesar the Dictator — 46
5. Antony and Cleopatra — 61
6. Antony Abandons Cleopatra — 77
7. Antony and Cleopatra Reunited — 85
8. The Warrior Queen — 99
9. The Battle of Actium — 105
10. Cleopatra's Death — 114
11. Aftermath — 127

Author's Note — 131
Chronology — 133
Notes — 136
Bibliography — 144
Index — 146

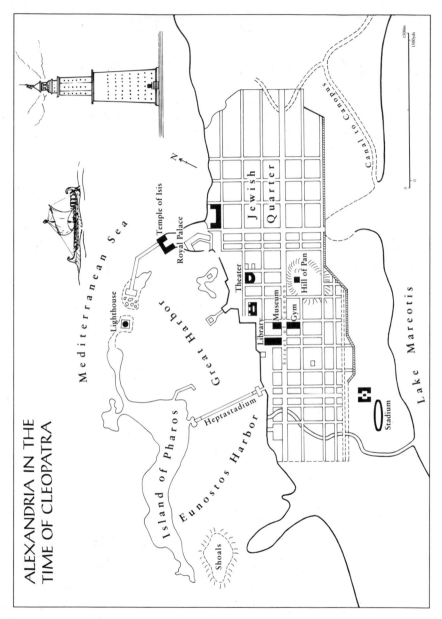

ALEXANDRIA IN THE
TIME OF CLEOPATRA

Plan of Alexandria. Note causeway built to join Pharos Island to
the mainland, creating two harbors. A canal at the north end of
the causeway allowed boats to pass from one harbor to the other.
The lighthouse is at the northeastern tip of the island.

INTRODUCTION

∿∿∿∿∿∿∿∿∿∿∿

CLEOPATRA'S WORLD

*For her actual beauty was not itself
remarkable . . . but the contact of her presence . . .
was irresistible; the attraction of her person,
joining with the charm of her conversation . . .
was something bewitching. It was a pleasure
merely to hear her voice, with which, like an
instrument of many strings, she could pass
from one language to another.*
—PLUTARCH

T his was Cleopatra, Queen of Egypt, the most
famous queen of the ancient Greek and Roman
world. Even if not the perfection of beauty—
some thought her nose too large for her delicate little
body—her stunning personality inspired endless myths
and legends, as well as some of the greatest poets and
dramatists throughout the ages. There have been other
great queens in antiquity, but none can compare with
Cleopatra, who still intrigues and fascinates us today,
some 2000 years later.

Beyond her charm, Cleopatra was a powerful political

force, playing a crucial role at a crucial moment in history. She was a key figure in the clash between East and West, who were both struggling to control the Mediterranean world. Her western enemies, the Romans, feared her so much that they launched a vicious smear campaign to blacken her reputation; they painted her as an evil, lustful siren who lured men like their greatest leaders, Julius Caesar and Mark Antony, to destruction.

The Romans' one-sided portrayal of Cleopatra as a wicked, lustful manipulator made good press and was touted by historians, poets, and dramatists in the West, and it is this image we have inherited. Only a few isolated praises of the Queen's true accomplishments have survived.

Her Egyptian subjects worshipped Cleopatra as the divine goddess Isis, the caring mother of all mankind. To one Arab historian she was a "sage and a scholar." To an Egyptian dramatist she was a nationalistic heroine, defending her kingdom, Egypt, against Roman aggression. Unfortunately, most records of her accomplishments were destroyed by her enemies after her death.

No one can deny her allure, but her real passion in life was not lust for sex but preserving her country's independence. And even in the most vicious propaganda against her, a certain admiration for her courage, her brilliance, and her power shows through.

Though Queen of Egypt, Cleopatra was a Greek and had not one drop of Egyptian blood. She was the seventh queen named Cleopatra and the last monarch of a Macedonian Greek dynasty, the Ptolemies, who ruled the kingdom of Egypt for almost 300 years, from shortly after the death of Alexander the Great in 323 B.C. until the Queen's death in 30 B.C. She could boast a connection with the long-dead hero Alexander, Egypt's conqueror, for he was related to her direct ancestor, the first King Ptolemy.

Alexander's greatest legacy to the Ptolemies was the city Alexandria, named in his honor. From a tiny fishing village in the delta where the Nile River empties into the Mediterranean Sea, it became an unrivaled center of trade and Greek culture and, some thought, the most beautiful city in the world.

Though the capital of its subject kingdom, Egypt, which lay inland and south along the banks of the Nile River, Alexandria was more oriented to the north, the Mediterranean world. It attracted not only merchants but the greatest scholars of the day from Greece and the Near East.

Alexandria welcomed people of all races and tolerated all religions. The concept that only one religion was true and all others false never occurred to the Alexandrians. They realized that many gods and goddesses were basically the same, though known by different names. The attributes of Greek and Egyptian deities slowly began to merge in the popular mind.

The only group to suffer in this otherwise enlightened city of many nationalities was the working class, the native Egyptians who farmed the land, crafted glassware and jewelry, and wove fine linen for export—all to the profit of their Greek rulers. Treated as second-class citizens, bowed down by overwork and taxes, they often rose in revolt and staged violent strikes.

Cleopatra, who lived and died in Alexandria, knew all about her hardheaded, efficient Ptolemy forebears, who had brought the kingdom to its peak of glory and wealth. But by her time it was in sharp decline, its rulers grown weak and corrupt, unable to manage affairs of state. Internecine strife and quarrels over the right to the throne led to ruthless intrigues and murder. Ptolemy queens were as bloodthirsty as the kings, fighting like tigresses for their own and their children's power.

By the first century B.C., the weakened, decadent Ptolemy dynasty was faced with a threat from the West. This was Rome, capital of the Roman Republic in Italy. Rome, whose military might filled the East with terror, had been expanding its power overseas. Now it was coming closer and closer to Egypt, eager for the country's fabled wealth.

When Cleopatra was born, in 69 B.C., the shadow of Rome had deepened, and fear of its military aggression hung heavily on both Greeks and Egyptians, who despised the Romans—they thought them boorish, uneducated upstarts, only interested in the martial arts. In turn, the Romans thought Greeks and Egyptians effeminate and degenerate. There was a widespread ethnic hatred between the East and the West of the Mediterranean world.

As the menace of Rome increased, Cleopatra's city grew more and more turbulent. When she was still a little girl, an angry mob lynched a Roman visitor for killing a cat, an animal sacred to the Egyptians. Soon Princess Cleopatra began forming her own ideas of how she would handle the Romans when she grew up.

ONE

CLEOPATRA GROWS UP

*And while Rome will be hesitating over the
conquest of Egypt, then the mighty Queen
will appear among men.*
—SIBYLLINE ORACLE

Princess Cleopatra grew up in the luxury of the
royal palace in Alexandria, a vast cluster of Greek-
colonnaded buildings surrounded by beautiful
gardens full of flowering fruit trees and little ponds with
delicate blue-and-white lotus blossoms. The palace lay
close to the harbor and was cooled by sea breezes. It had
its own private, secluded landing area where the sound
of gently lapping water and the call of sea birds filled the
air. Nearby, on a rocky little island, rose a smaller
palace, a retreat for the royal family.

Within the palace long marbled corridors led to various

apartments—banquet and reception rooms, bedrooms with their private lavatories replete with running water. Huge kitchens were always busy with chefs preparing roasts and sweet delicacies. Fountains and flowering shrubs adorned interior courtyards, and outside balconies caught the evening breezes and gave views in all directions.

From her balcony, Cleopatra had a fine view of the city's famous lighthouse, Pharos, named for the island on which it stood. It was the pride of Alexandria and considered one of the Seven Wonders of the World. Rising to a height of 500 feet, it was topped by a glass lantern. Here a bright flame from a huge fire kept burning day and night was reflected by mirrors and was visible far out to sea, welcoming ships to the safety of the city's wonderful deep harbor.

Cleopatra could easily walk from her palace to the nearby museum and the famous library, with its collection of some 400,000 papyrus scrolls, comprising all the great literature of the Mediterranean world. A theater overlooked the harbor from a high ridge, while below sprawled the huge gymnasium cherished by the Greeks, who felt physical training was an important part of education. All these public buildings were of different-colored stone and marble. Carefully polished, they glistened in the brilliant sunshine under Egypt's cloudless skies.

There was also a zoological garden, which the Ptolemies had built for people to observe and enjoy exotic animals— unlike the Romans, who put on wild-beast shows in order to hunt and kill animals.

Cleopatra's father, King Ptolemy XII, and his six children—Cleopatra, her two older sisters, a younger half-sister, and two little half-brothers—also lived in the palace. Cleopatra's mother had died when Cleopatra was very young, and her father had remarried. Each child had a separate apartment; each had his or her own servants and guardians to protect them and see to their education.

There was not much love between the children. They all tried to outshine one another in a kind of race to win the power of the throne. This fierce competition was encouraged by their ambitious guardians, who were eager for their share of royal power and therefore shamelessly egged on their charges. As a result the children grew up in an atmosphere of palace intrigue, corruption, and devious schemes to get to the top.

Away from the secretive and evil plotting in her palace, Cleopatra found more pleasurable diversions. One of her youthful delights was the elaborate festival honoring the popular joy-giving god Dionysus. Though most famous as the god of wine, Dionysus was also the god of the arts, of music, dance, and drama. People loved his festival for its wine drinking, music, and dancing—it made them forget their cares and anxieties. No one loved these revels more than Cleopatra's father, King Ptolemy.

A weak ruler and a strange, enigmatic man, the King had a passion for playing the flute as well as a fondness for wine. Though he had the honorary title of the "New Dionysus"—all the Ptolemy monarchs were honored with divine titles, both for prestige and in order to impress

Bust of Cleopatra's father, the "Flute Player." He is wearing the ivy wreath of the god Dionysus.

the people—Cleopatra's father did not impress the people. They found him neither kingly nor godly and called him the "Flute Player." He often joined the musicians and dancers in the Dionysian festivals, and Cleopatra could see her father playing his flute and dancing through the city streets in a most unregal way. Fond of dancing, music,

and drama herself—she had a flair for putting on shows—
Cleopatra found no fault with her father's behavior,
although it may have bothered her to see how little his
subjects respected him. She knew he was shrewd and
intelligent, if not strong, and had done much for his
kingdom in repairing old buildings and temples and
creating new ones. He supported the arts and learning
and passed on his special interest in philosophy to
Cleopatra, thought to be his favorite daughter.

Cleopatra had an unusually good education. At a very
young age she learned the stories and myths of the Greek
and Egyptian gods and goddesses. She undoubtedly
picked up bits of Egyptian lore from her Egyptian women
servants. She was especially drawn to the Egyptian
goddess Isis, believed to have power over heaven and
earth, but whose greatest appeal was her compassion,
mercy, and concern for women and children.

Princess Cleopatra was quick and eager to learn, and
as she grew older, she went on to more advanced literature, the arts, science and medicine, and the study of
many languages. She was the first Ptolemy to bother to
learn the native Egyptian tongue so as to be able to communicate with her Egyptian subjects. She also knew
Arabic and Hebrew and could talk to the many Jews
who had settled in Alexandria. At the museum (really an
academy for scholarly research) she talked to scientists
and doctors, to philosophers and writers. Like her father
she was interested in philosophy, especially the philosophy of governing that sought to justify kingship and to
demonstrate how to be a strong yet benevolent ruler.

Bust of Cleopatra, once but no longer thought to be authentic, since the hairdo differs from Cleopatra's style. But it seems to suggest her resemblance to her father, as do coins depicting the Queen.

The scholars residing in Alexandria were all aware that they were entirely supported by the royalty. Often they had to lay aside their own research to satisfy the whims of the royal family. They might suddenly be called upon to produce poems of praise for the King or Queen, medical prescriptions, cosmetics, engines of war, or mechanical toys for festivals and gala events.

But beyond her joys in learning and celebrating the many festivals, Cleopatra was worried about her kingdom's decline, and kept thinking of its past glory. Her own name meant "glory to her race," and Cleopatra became obsessed with the idea of restoring Egypt's great past and power. But how could one stop the growing menace of Rome?

Cleopatra knew how inadequate the Egyptian army was and that recent Ptolemy kings had felt forced to appeal to Rome for military help to control the sporadic outbreaks of the Alexandrian mobs. There was even a rumor that Cleopatra's grandfather had willed Egypt to Rome in exchange for helping him to keep his throne. He was soon found murdered by the Alexandrian mob. Cleopatra vowed that when she grew up, she would not let the Romans use her or make her country a Roman province—rather, she would use them in any way she could to make Egypt the proud leader of the Mediterranean world it once had been.

But now her unpopular father was having trouble, as the populace again grew more and more unruly and menacing. With no strong army to back him, and fearing to lose his throne—perhaps even his life, as his father had—he too decided to go to Rome for help. Cleopatra found this humiliating, but she admired her father's shrewdness. She knew it was wiser for the survival of both the kingdom and himself to seek Rome's support rather than to risk confronting its armies.

Cleopatra was only ten when her father set off for Rome, but her precocious interest in politics made her curious to know how he would deal with the Romans and what he could accomplish.

Though nation after nation was falling to Rome's military might, the Roman Republic was having its own troubles. Equally as corrupt as Egypt, its republican government was on the verge of collapse. Three power-hungry politicians, Julius Caesar, Pompey, and Crassus, using bribery and voter intimidation, had all but seized control of the government, making a mockery of republican institutions.

Almost five hundred years earlier the Romans had dispensed with monarchy and set up a republic, a government of checks and balances with two annually elected consuls (like presidents), a senate (lawmakers), and the citizens (the voters). But Rome's recent expansion, its military successes, and its new wealth from conquered lands were undermining its republican ideals. Army men and military heroes began to dominate the government; greedy for the wealth of the rich East, they focused their thoughts on further conquests.

Egypt, with its fabled wealth, had become a hot political issue, a prize coveted by Caesar, Pompey, and Crassus. But all three agreed that for the present it would be best to make deals to keep Egypt happy. Should they grab it now, they feared that whoever was sent to govern it would exploit the kingdom's wealth for himself and threaten their own power. So when Cleopatra's father appeared in Rome in 59 B.C., the three of them made a deal with the Flute Player. In exchange for a huge bribe, a sum almost equal to Egypt's yearly income, they agreed to support his claim to

the throne. Further they demanded immediate payment—
and they were not men to argue with. So the King turned
to a Roman moneylender to borrow the money to pay the
Romans to keep him on the throne of Egypt! Of course, he
would have to repay this debt eventually, and that would
not be easy. He knew that his subjects hated the Romans
even more than they hated him.

But, for the moment, the King was happy, assured by
Caesar that he was indeed the rightful King of Egypt and
"a friend and ally of the Roman people."

Cleopatra was twelve years old when her father returned to Alexandria with the decree that he was the
rightful King of Egypt. But no sooner was he back on his
throne than disheartening news reached him—Rome had
taken over the rich island of Cyprus, Egypt's only remaining overseas possession. Added to this stab in the
back, the King learned that the island's royal treasure of
priceless jewels and gold had been shipped to Rome and
displayed in the Forum, the city's famous center where
people gathered for business, politics, and celebrations.
The Flute Player's brother, who was the King of Cyprus,
committed suicide rather than submit to Roman rule.

The annexation of Cyprus happened just as the Flute
Player was beginning to tax his subjects to repay his
great debt to Rome. The people grew angry—angry at
being taxed, angry at their King for not helping his
brother resist the Roman takeover of Cyprus. A rebellion
broke out, and the King was forced to flee. Having less
pride than his brother, he again set off to Rome for help.

Was Egypt going to lose its independence to the

superpower, Rome? Such thoughts must have worried Cleopatra, but more immediate horrors in the palace now absorbed her. In her father's absence, her oldest sister seized the throne, only to be murdered when her next-oldest sister, Berenice, backed by palace intriguers and the Alexandrian mob, took her place.

We don't know what Cleopatra thought of this, but she was loyal to and fond of her father; such an insult to him probably enraged her. For her young age, she was getting a tough, sordid education in the reality of the politics of her world, an education very different from her more intellectual training. With her mother dead and her father away, she had no caring person to guide her moral values. She had to create her own, just as she had already formed her own ideas of how to deal with Rome. Rome might be trying to break Egypt's spirit, but it would not break hers.

In Rome her father managed one more deal, this time with Pompey alone. Pompey was home glorying in his military triumphs over Syria and Judaea. Caesar, not to be outdone, was off in the west, conquering Gaul (now France); and Crassus was boldly attacking the great Parthian Empire (now Iraq and Iran). Conquered long ago by Alexander the Great, Parthia had regained independence and was menacing Roman provinces. This vast area would add enormous glory to the Roman who could capture it. Every leader in the Mediterranean world wanted to become the new Alexander the Great.

For the moment, however, Pompey was the hero of the day and making the most of his popularity in Rome. With a shrewd eye to gaining the wealth of Egypt for himself someday, Pompey now promised Cleopatra's father military support, to put him back on his throne. Though the Flute Player had to pay an even larger bribe than his earlier one, he returned to Alexandria followed by Roman soldiers plucked from Pompey's legions stationed in Syria, his most recent conquest.

Leading these Roman soldiers was a young, handsome legionnaire, Mark Antony. He seemed a very Hercules of a man, with his powerful build and a face that spelled courage and confidence. In fact, Antony *did* resemble paintings and statues of the god-hero Hercules and liked to claim that his family was descended from him. Antony stayed only a short time in Alexandria, but long enough to meet Cleopatra, now fourteen, whose charm and delightful way of speaking he would not forget.

Restored to power for a second time, Cleopatra's father now had to deal with his daughter Berenice, who had usurped his throne. It was quickly done—he had her put to death for treason. Then he began anew the unpopular task of squeezing taxes from the people to repay his increasing debt to the Romans.

This time, with Roman legions on hand, the people could not openly rebel, but they seethed inwardly, angry and resentful. As Rome was slowly repaid, an uneasy peace descended on Alexandria for a few years. The King went back to playing his flute and reveling in Dionysian orgies. But the people knew only too well that their kingdom was becoming a mere puppet state under the control of far-off Rome.

In 51 B.C. the King died. He had willed his throne jointly to his oldest remaining daughter, Cleopatra, now eighteen, and to his ten-year-old son, Ptolemy. Cleopatra would be Cleopatra VII, Ptolemy would be Ptolemy XIII. Cleopatra had hoped to avoid marrying her little half-brother, but the old custom of brother-sister marriages in the royal family was too entrenched. It had become the rule for royalty, and her brother's three guardians wouldn't let her get away with such independence.

The Ptolemies had adopted the ancient custom of royal intermarriages from the Egyptians, along with their use of divine titles—ancient Egyptian pharaohs were all considered divine. Such brother-sister marriages were elitist, devised to prevent any commoner from contaminating the royal family, as well as to maintain the loyalty and respect of their subjects. Native Egyptians, especially the priestly class, would have been horrified to have any king or queen give up royal purity or divinity by marrying outside the royal family. Even before she became Queen, Cleopatra was considered a goddess and was expected to marry her equally divine brother.

Generations of inbreeding may well have caused weaknesses to appear in the Ptolemy line, but it could also sharpen good qualities, as Cleopatra, who was anything but weak or stupid, seemed to prove.

So Cleopatra dutifully, if reluctantly, married her little brother. Though the marriage was nothing more than a formality, the wedding was splendid. There were two marriage ceremonies: one Greek, with Cleopatra dressed as the Greek goddess of love, Aphrodite, and her little brother as Dionysus. The other was Egyptian, with Cleopatra as the goddess Isis and her brother as Isis's

Slave girls putting makeup on a lady.

consort, Osiris, god of the Nile River. No one loved a pageant more than Cleopatra, whose artistic talents now revealed her flair for showmanship.

Any disappointment in marrying her brother was temporarily dispelled as she dressed up as goddess Isis, for she, the Queen, now bore the title of the "New Isis," beloved above all other goddesses. Her gossamer robe was of brilliant colors, red, yellow, and white, edged with a band of delicately woven fruits and flowers. A shiny black cape, embroidered with gold stars and a fiery red moon, was gracefully draped over her shoulders. Her royal Egyptian crown was topped by a cobra, the sacred serpent of the Nile. Added to her shimmering costume was the allure of her makeup. Cleopatra was skilled in the art of cosmetics, the use of eye pencil, eye shadow, and skin lotions, an art perfected by Egyptians long before and taught to her by her female servants. She also used the most delicate and expensive perfumes, imported from Arabia and far-off India.

Despite the emphasis on brother-sister rule, it was not long before Cleopatra was ruling as though she were the one and only monarch, much to the anger of her brother and his guardians. Already they were teaching the boy King to hate and envy his sister Queen. But the Queen knew that her ten-year-old brother was not capable of coping with the problems she had inherited. Aside from the ever-present menace of Rome and the unrest in Alexandria, times in Egypt were hard. The Nile River had failed to produce its annual flooding, that amazing phenomenon on which the whole country depended. When the waters of the Nile failed to rise over and nourish and enrich the soil along the river's edge, few crops would grow and starvation threatened the people.

So it happened in Cleopatra's first year as Queen. Famine set in, the poor grew poorer. To avoid the hated tax collectors, many took to hiding out in the desert. Knowing of the unrest south of Alexandria, in Upper Egypt, the land where Egypt's ancient civilization had developed thousands of years earlier, Cleopatra made a bold decision. She would go off without her brother-consort or his guardians to see for herself what Egyptian life was like beyond the confines of her city. It would be a most unusual adventure for a Greek.

TWO

~~~~~~~~~~~~~~~~~~~

CLEOPATRA'S VISIT TO THE NILE

O Nile, verdant art thou, who makest
man and cattle to live.
—OLD HYMN TO THE NILE RIVER

nlike her unkingly father, Cleopatra was every inch a queen and deeply committed to her royal responsibilities and her role as the Goddess Isis. She now set off on her first goodwill tour to the southern part of her kingdom, Upper Egypt, a land she had never seen. From her royal barge, which carried her south by canal to the Nile River, she could see all kinds of boats: rowboats, sailboats, and barges laden with grain and raw materials, visible signs of the hardworking tillers of the soil.

Once on the beautiful Nile River she seemed to be in another world. The longest river in the world, the Nile flows north from its source deep in the heart of Africa for four thousand miles and empties into the Mediterranean Sea near Alexandria. Egypt proper lies along only about one fourth of this expanse.

Cleopatra had been taught the history of Egypt as well as its ancient myths. Though she probably had no idea how long the Nile River was, she knew the myth of its creation—how the grief-stricken goddess Isis couldn't stop shedding tears for her murdered husband, Osiris, until, after many years, she found all his severed parts. Legend claimed that she wept so long and copiously that her tears created the Nile River!

But Cleopatra may not have been prepared for the sight of so many wondrous buildings and huge statues— the imposing pyramids, the sphinx with its lion's body and a human head, and slender obelisks of gigantic height, each made of one huge block of stone weighing tons. How could the ancient Egyptians have transported these huge monoliths from quarries some five hundred miles away? It all seemed unbelievable and remote from her Greek world.

No sooner had Cleopatra set foot on land than she was hailed as the "New Goddess Isis, the Queen, the Lady of Two Lands," and asked to lead a religious ceremony on the river itself. It was an unusual ceremony to a Greek, but one long hallowed by the Egyptians.

A sacred bull, believed to embody the soul of the great sun god, Re, had died and had to be replaced by a new one. Since Re was the divine father of the goddess Isis, and since Cleopatra wanted to make the most of her royal title of the New Isis, she was honored to lead the procession. She also knew it was politically wise to show her respect for the ancient and revered Egyptian gods and goddesses and to keep on good terms with the highly esteemed priests of Re.

So the Queen, along with the priests and a young black bull, was rowed up the Nile in a ceremonial barge to the god's temple, where the new bull would be installed. When the bull was safely in his temple, people gave thanks and sang hymns to the god Re, who dwelt in the bull's body; the faithful were convinced that he would nourish and protect them. The festive ceremony ended with the loud music of harps and flutes and with wild rejoicing.

From time immemorial Egyptians had been in close touch with nature and animal life. They knew instinctively that every living creature, from beetle to bull, contributed to nature and man. The ritual of the bull went back to primitive times, when people wanted some visible sign from an unseen god. Their respect for animals led them to depict their unseen gods as animals, or humans with animal heads. Since the great sun god Re was their most powerful god, the source of life itself, it was natural for him to dwell in an animal of great strength, such as a bull.

It was easy to make fun of this "beastial" religion, as the Romans and others did, taunting Egyptians for worshipping beasts instead of gods. But the basic idea was

Ceremonial riverboat such as Cleopatra may have used on her first Nile trip to install the sacred bull.

little different from the Greek and Roman worship of statues of their gods—likewise visible symbols of unseen gods.

Cleopatra didn't taunt her subjects and respected their desire to cling to their ancient religious rituals, which had served them so well for so long. Earlier Ptolemy monarchs had paid little attention to such ceremonies, except occasionally to send deputies to represent the royal court. Cleopatra was likely the first Ptolemy to partake in, as well as to lead, such a ceremony. Her expedition was, of course, good public relations and greatly enhanced her popularity among her Egyptian subjects. But, back in her Greek city, Alexandria, she was anything but popular.

Upon returning home, Cleopatra found a growing discontent with her actions. When the Roman governor of Syria asked for the return of his soldiers who had come to help her father, Cleopatra politely agreed and ordered them back. By this time, however, many of these soldiers had married Alexandrian women, and were enjoying the city's pleasures and comforts. They had forgotten their Roman discipline and now thought of themselves more as Alexandrians than as Romans. They refused to leave, and murdered the messengers sent to demand their return.

Cleopatra promptly arrested the murderers and sent them back to the Roman governor of Syria. Incensed, the remaining soldiers joined the excitable city mob, who felt that Cleopatra's dealings with the Roman governor of Syria smacked of pro-Roman sympathy and that she was showing signs of her father's pro-Roman policy.

Far worse, a plot to get rid of the Queen was being hatched by the three guardians of her younger brother, who were scheming to gain control of the throne for themselves. The most artful and devious of these guardians was the fat eunuch Pothinus, minister of finance. Another was the army commander, and the third was young Ptolemy's tutor. If they could remove Cleopatra, they knew they could easily manage the little boy King Ptolemy. They already knew they could never control the

Queen, whose independence was showing more and more every day. The three guardians, too, suspected Cleopatra of continuing her father's pro-Roman policy—at least that was their excuse in trying to depose her.

Getting wind of the plot to depose her, perhaps even to murder her, Cleopatra, as her father before her, was forced to flee, and her brother was proclaimed sole ruler of Egypt.

How Cleopatra managed to escape is a mystery, as no records survive of what must have been a hazardous adventure for the young Queen. All we know is that she ended up in the nearby Roman province of Syria with only a small band of loyal followers.

During Cleopatra's absence, the scheming royal guardians felt free to mold young Ptolemy as they wished. They felt sure they were now the power behind the throne; but they hadn't reckoned with the shrewdness, determination, and ambition of a young queen equally schooled in the ruthless craftiness of the palace.

Using her knowledge of Hebrew and Arabic to communicate, and her charm to persuade, Cleopatra managed to gather an army to march against her brother. She was confident she would win and soon be Queen again. Then she would fulfill her ambition to build up Egypt's power to its former glory. She planned to be a queen on equal footing with Roman leaders, not just their footstool, as her father had been.

THREE

~~~~~~~~~~~~~~~~~~~~~~~~~~

CLEOPATRA MEETS CAESAR

He saw the Egyptian wealth with greedy eyes,
And wished some fair pretence to seize the prize.
—ROMAN POET LUCAN

The scheming that went on in Alexandria's palace was matched in faraway Rome by an equally ruthless struggle for power. The Triumvirate—the joint rule of three power-hungry men, Julius Caesar, Pompey, and Crassus—had collapsed in 53 B.C., when Crassus was killed attacking the Parthians in the Middle East. Now a struggle between Caesar and Pompey had developed.

Caesar returned to Italy in 49 B.C., after spectacular military successes in the vast lands of Gaul. He was the supreme military hero of the moment, and war was in his heart when he and his legions came back to Italy. Disregarding the centuries-old law of the Roman Republic, he refused to disband his army before entering the capital city, Rome. He was heading for a showdown with Pompey, who had rallied Caesar's political enemies, especially those Romans who feared that Caesar would use his military power to gain sole control of the Republic.

As Caesar advanced on Rome, Pompey retreated and headed for northern Greece, hoping for support from the eastern provinces he had conquered and preparing to make a stand against his former colleague.

Caesar was soon ready to pursue his old ally, now his bitter foe. The two armies clashed on a plain in northern Greece. It quickly became a rout, as Caesar's seasoned legions demolished Pompey's forces in the bloodiest battle ever fought among Romans. Pompey managed to escape, fleeing south across the Mediterranean Sea for Alexandria.

He expected a warm reception there—hadn't he helped Cleopatra's father regain his throne? Wouldn't the new monarchs of Egypt, the boy King Ptolemy and his sister, Queen Cleopatra, lend a helping hand? Pompey thought of himself as a friend and ally of Egypt. He didn't know that Cleopatra had been forced to leave Alexandria and that a war between brother and sister was imminent.

When the Alexandrians heard of Pompey's approach, the boy King's guardians decided it would be wiser to make peace with the new great military hero of the hour, Julius Caesar, and get rid of the loser, Pompey.

Young King Ptolemy's military commander was chosen for the job. As soon as Pompey's galley dropped

anchor in the harbor, the commander and two soldiers rowed out to escort Pompey to shore. Pompey's wife was on board the galley and, sensing that all was not right, tried to persuade her husband not to go. But Pompey was already in the little landing boat. As he was about to step ashore, he was struck down, stabbed in the back. Then, as his wife watched in horror from the galley, the murderers cut off Pompey's head! The ship's crew immediately raised anchor and headed for the open sea, leaving only the echo of a woman's screams.

Caesar arrived four days later.

The murderers were wrong. Caesar was not at all pleased when they presented him with Pompey's severed head. In fact it was said he wept at the sight. It was one thing to kill an enemy in honorable battle, quite another to have him treacherously murdered by these scheming Alexandrians.

Caesar had arrived in Alexandria with only ten ships and a small force of foot soldiers. The Alexandrians had expected that Caesar, with his enemy Pompey out of the way, would return to Rome immediately. To linger in this turbulent city amid its angry mob with only a small force of soldiers was highly risky. But the self-confident Caesar enjoyed taking risks. And, much to the horror of the Alexandrians, he moved into the palace and made himself at home.

Neither Cleopatra nor her brother Ptolemy was in the

Bust of Julius Caesar showing lines of age but not his lack of hair.

palace. Cleopatra was approaching Egypt's frontier, thirty miles east of Alexandria, with the army she had raised while in Syria during her absence of several months. Alerted of her approach, young Ptolemy, led by his guardians, had gone to confront her. The war between brother and sister was beginning.

Sizing up the situation, Caesar, like Pompey, remembered his past help to Cleopatra's father, as well as his promise to carry out the King's will: Cleopatra and her brother were to rule *jointly*. He would stop this war between siblings and be the arbiter to reestablish their joint rule. Caesar never doubted his own schemes nor his ability to carry them out.

Then, as he observed the fabulous display of wealth and luxury surrounding him in the beautiful palace—its alabaster walls, its carved ivory balustrades, its mosaic floors with elaborate scenes—he also remembered that Rome had not been fully repaid the money loaned to Cleopatra's father. Caesar was always in need of money, another compelling reason to remain in this mad city.

The Alexandrians were already rioting, enraged that a hated Roman had the effrontery to move into the royal palace as though he were in command of the city. The treacherous murder of Pompey had not worked out as they had hoped.

Caesar moved quickly. He summoned young Ptolemy to appear before him. This, of course, infuriated Ptolemy's guardians, especially Pothinus, but Caesar's summons was duly obeyed. Despite his small army he seemed to inspire fear. He then sent a message to Cleopatra to return.

Unlike her brother, the Queen was only too eager for this chance to talk to the great Caesar and present her case. Confident that she could work things out to her advantage, she was soon on her way.

It was a dangerous undertaking—the frontier was still blocked by her brother's army and Alexandria's harbor by his ships. But Cleopatra was never at a loss for ideas, and she, too, enjoyed taking risks. She called on a loyal follower, a Sicilian merchant, to row her to her palace in a small skiff.

Dusk had fallen as they slipped past Ptolemy's fleet and rowed quietly to the palace's private landing. To get into the palace unnoticed, Cleopatra had the merchant conceal her in a carpet. Tying up his bundle, he slung it over his shoulders and carried it up the marble stairway into the palace and past guards who probably thought it just a rug delivery for Caesar. Admitted to Caesar's apartment, the merchant laid his bundle carefully on the floor and opened it. Cleopatra, more disheveled than usual, emerged, much to the amazement of the suave, usually self-contained Caesar.

To have the Queen arrive in this unexpected manner was indeed a shock, but apparently a delightful one. Caesar, now aged fifty-two, was still handsome, with good features and piercing dark eyes. He had long been a womanizer, and here was a twenty-one-year-old queen who seemed not only enchanting but unusual. Caesar was sure of his own appeal to women. When not on the battlefield, he was quite a dandy and cared a great deal about his looks. He kept his body lean and muscular. He had one worry—baldness. He often wore his victory wreath to conceal it. He was clean shaven and even had his body hairs plucked out by his barber.

Caesar and Cleopatra seem to have been attracted to each other right away. Cleopatra's melodious voice, her daring—so like his own—her wit and intelligence, delighted him. And she was equally impressed by Caesar's bearing, his intelligence, and his self-confidence. Caesar was no typical boorish Roman barbarian but a cultivated man of the world—he could even talk to her in Greek.

There was another compelling reason for their desire for each other—their similar ambitions to rule the world. That Caesar was now the most powerful commander in the Mediterranean world was part of his charm for Cleopatra. That Cleopatra belonged to a splendid royal dynasty connected with Alexander the Great and was Queen of the wealthiest country in this same world was, perhaps, an even greater attraction for Caesar. Cleopatra was confident that this great military hero could restore her to power, and he was sure that the glittering prize of Egypt was his for the future. They became lovers almost immediately.

When young Ptolemy, now thirteen, was summoned to Caesar's presence the day after his sister's arrival, he was shocked to find the two together. He rushed from the room, shouting he had been betrayed. Once in the street, he tore off his crown and hurled it to the ground in a violent rage. Crowds gathered and surged menacingly toward the palace. But Caesar's bodyguard got the boy

King back inside while Caesar himself calmed the people, promising to settle things.

Caesar now showed his skill as a politician. At a lavish banquet replete with the palace gold plates and delicate glass goblets, with background music of flutes and harps, he announced that Cleopatra and Ptolemy were reconciled as Queen and King of Egypt. (Secretly he must have had no doubts who would have the upper hand.) He then announced that the island of Cyprus, recently annexed by the Romans, would be returned to Egypt and ruled jointly by Cleopatra's younger sister and youngest brother. He knew this would be popular with the Alexandrians, though it would hardly please the Romans. The gesture caused a slight lull in the hostilities, and Caesar was able to enjoy Cleopatra's company and her beautiful city.

The library and museum and the many scholars from Greece and other countries impressed him. It was probably Cleopatra who introduced him to the astronomer Sosigenes, who explained to him the solar calendar of 365 days, far more accurate than the Roman calendar based on a lunar year of 355 days, which caused the record of the seasons to get out of order. Some of the greatest Greek scientists had worked at the museum for scientific research, anticipating by 1,500 years the discoveries of Copernicus and Galileo. Medical research was far advanced, and the city could boast a public health system, possibly the first in the world, to provide medical assistance for all and strict supervision of hygiene.

From an artificial conelike hill, built just for the purpose of a good view, Cleopatra could show Caesar the entire city, the well-laid-out avenues lined with palm trees, the marble temples and stone buildings, the lush, tropical gardens, the canals teeming with boats, and the sparkling freshwater lake that supplied drinking water for the inhabitants.

Caesar must have been pleased to see a new temple being built in his honor at the Queen's request. Called the Caesarium, its entrance was graced by two ancient obelisks from Upper Egypt. Known now as Cleopatra's Needles, they are familiar sights, one in London, the other in New York's Central Park.

Looking north, Cleopatra and Caesar had a fine view of the harbor and its famed lighthouse, the Pharos. In addition to sending forth its powerful beacon of light, this engineering masterpiece supplied weather information through the movement of mechanical statues near the top. One statue, following the sun's course, marked the hours of the day; another indicated the direction of the wind; a third was designed to sound an alarm at the approach of an enemy!

Caesar's city of Rome seemed backward and provincial in comparison. No wonder Cleopatra was proud of Alexandria and her inheritance.

If the royal family outwardly seemed reconciled, the boy King's chief guardian, Pothinus, certainly was not. He did not trust Caesar and resented his taking over the position of arbiter of the royal court. Pothinus considered himself the top official in Alexandria; he thought that he should be the one to make all decisions for the royal family. But here was this outsider, and a Roman to boot, intervening in Ptolemy affairs without even consulting him. The only solution was to get rid of Caesar. To carry out his plot, he secretly ordered young Ptolemy's army to return from the frontier and besiege the palace, by both land and sea.

Caesar was now surrounded and outnumbered five to one. He was in a dangerous position, but he knew that the Alexandrian army was largely made up of a motley group of runaway slaves, outlaws, and pirates, unequal to his disciplined soldiers. He had, however, overlooked the guile of the Alexandrians. They managed to pump briny seawater into the freshwater conduits leading to the palace compound, making the water undrinkable. Even Caesar's tough legionnaires could not fight without drinking water. So Caesar set his men to digging wells by night, and fresh water was discovered near the shore. Then the fighting began in earnest, as the Alexandrians started to assault the palace and bring their fleet into the harbor.

Cleopatra watched the battle from her palace window and could see the large Egyptian fleet assembling. Right away, Caesar outsmarted his enemy, sending his small fleet out from the inner harbor of the palace to surprise the Egyptian sailors just as they were lowering anchors. Every ship was captured and then set on fire. Cleopatra saw the entire Egyptian fleet burst into flames. Then came a more alarming sight, as the flames from the burning ships leaped onto the docks and harbor warehouses. One, full of precious scrolls, burned to the ground.

But Caesar's sudden capture of the enemy fleet enabled him, that same day, to attack and secure the island and

Pharos Lighthouse.
Memories of this
"Wonder of the
World" continued
long after its
disappearance,
as this modern
romanticized
engraving shows.

its precious lighthouse. Though Cleopatra may have worried about the scrolls lost in the fire, she was greatly relieved to see that Caesar had everything under control for the moment.

While Cleopatra was anxiously watching the harbor battle at one end of the palace, Pothinus was plotting behind closed doors at the other end. He managed to sneak Cleopatra's young half-sister, Arsinoë, out to join the rebel army, which promptly proclaimed her Queen of Egypt! Pothinus planned to follow with young Ptolemy for an all-out attack on Caesar. But the plot leaked out, picked up by Caesar's barber, who when not shaving his master was apparently an expert at eavesdropping.

On getting the news, Caesar acted quickly. He had Pothinus arrested and put to death for treason. The worst of the palace intriguers was out of the way. Soon afterward, the Egyptian army commander was murdered by a local rival gang. Arsinoë's guardians now took command and stepped up the attack on Caesar by bringing a new fleet into the harbor. (Egypt seemed to have an endless supply of ships.)

Luckily for Caesar, his own flotilla of reinforcements from Greece now began to arrive. As the fighting became more intense, Cleopatra had one more agonizing crisis to watch from her palace window. (Unlike any other war Caesar had fought, this one had the unusual feature of allowing him to fight within view of his mistress and to join her for dinner after the day's battle.)

Caesar was out on the causeway that connected Pharos Island with the mainland, directing his soldiers in building barricades to seal off the approach from the city, when suddenly the enemy landed on the island end of the causeway and attacked the Romans from behind. The motley Alexandrian army, which Caesar so scorned, was not so incompetent after all.

The Romans panicked, hastily abandoned their work, and scrambled to board the nearest ships. Cleopatra could see Caesar, dressed in full armor, plunge into the harbor from an overcrowded ship just before it sank. Anxious, but full of admiration, the Queen saw him swim in his heavy armor for about two hundred yards to the safety of another ship. He had to swim most of the way underwater to avoid the constant onslaught of enemy missiles. His only loss was his purple cape, picked up with glee by one of the enemy. It had been a close call, and Caesar very nearly lost his life. Some four hundred of his soldiers did.

Though fighting in the city continued, Caesar allowed young Ptolemy to leave the palace, fully expecting him to quarrel with his sister Arsinoë and cause dissension among the Alexandrians.

Instead, Ptolemy escaped and was nowhere to be found. While a search for him went on, Caesar's relieving land army finally appeared at the frontier. When Caesar joined it, they easily routed the rebel forces and ended the strange little war.

It was later learned that the boy King had joined other fugitives who had boarded an overcrowded ship on the Nile. When it sank, young Ptolemy, weighted down by his gold armor, drowned. Unlike the fifty-two-year-old

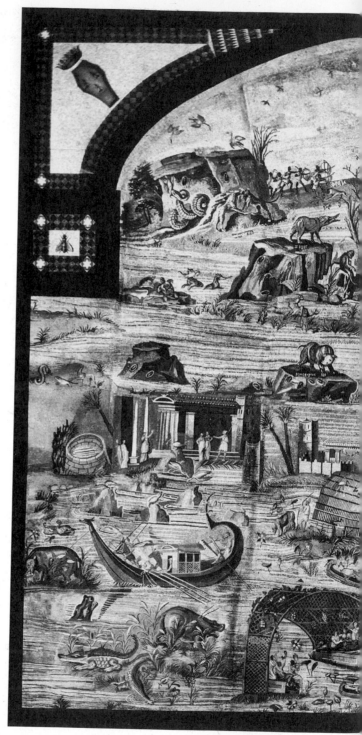

Nile River scenes from a Roman mosaic.

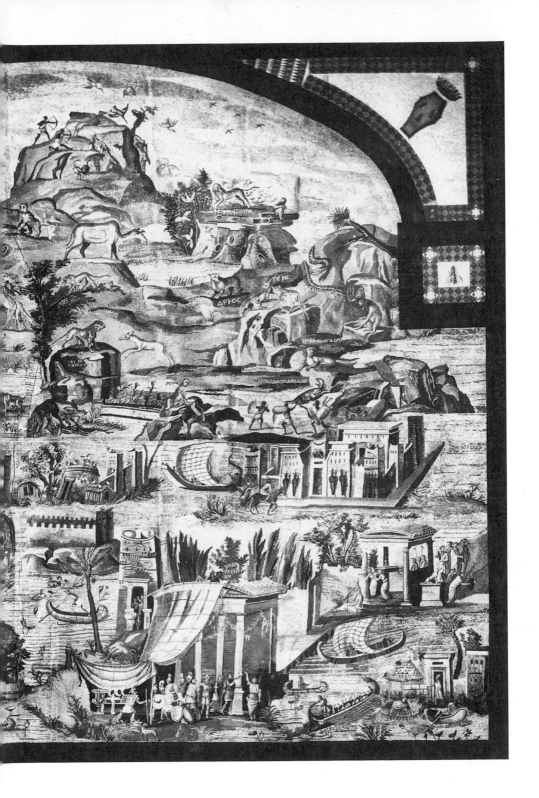

Caesar, he didn't have the strength to swim in heavy armor. The only consolation for his followers was that a certain glory was attached to dying in the sacred Nile.

Once again Caesar tried to regulate the royal family. He arrested Arsinoë as a treacherous troublemaker and then, in keeping with local tradition, arranged to have Cleopatra marry her youngest surviving half brother, twelve-year-old Ptolemy XIV. Cleopatra paid even less attention to this brother-husband co-ruler than she had to his older brother.

To further cement Cleopatra's restoration to the throne, Caesar joined her in a trip up the Nile. Leading the procession of several hundred boats, the couple relaxed in splendid luxury on board Cleopatra's royal barge. Made of cypress and cedar, it was 300 feet long and 60 feet high, and equipped with sails and several banks of oars. It was like a floating palace with elegant rooms and even gardens.

As Cleopatra had on her earlier Nile trip, Caesar observed the beauties of the Nile River, the green and fertile fields stretching from the river's edge, the feathery papyrus growing everywhere, and the extraordinary temples and monuments built for the everlasting glory of pharaoh god-rulers. When Cleopatra was hailed as the goddess Isis, Caesar may well have thought of himself as her divine royal consort, the god Osiris. Cleopatra was now pregnant, and the possibility of a son must have pleased Caesar, whose only child, a daughter, had died.

However infatuated Caesar was with Cleopatra, he knew it was time to leave, to tend to Roman affairs. He knew he had a competent, trustworthy ally in Cleopatra, and he left her three Roman legions (fifteen to twenty thousand men) for protection. Whatever emotions Cleopatra felt for Caesar, she knew her intimacy with him gave her hope that her dreams would come true— she would at last be able to reestablish Ptolemy rule and revive its past glories. She began right away seeing to her own administrative duties and maintaining a good relationship with her subjects. Now that the palace was temporarily rid of plotters, Cleopatra was freer to put her mind to ruling.

Not long after Caesar's departure, Cleopatra gave birth to a son, whom the Alexandrians nicknamed Caesarion, or little Caesar. She preferred to call him Ptolemy Caesar, expecting that he would carry on Ptolemy rule after her death. That he was born on a feast day of the goddess Isis was a good omen and pleased her Egyptian subjects.

Cleopatra began minting coins showing herself as the beloved goddess Isis, nursing her baby, Caesarion, just as the goddess had often been depicted nursing her own divine son. The same scene, in larger-than-life figures, soon appeared on temples. Caesarion had become divine. The Egyptians accepted his father, Caesar, as Cleopatra's divine husband, joined to her in a sacred marriage.

The Queen made the most of her role as the New Isis at the very time when the goddess's popularity had spread to the far corners of the Mediterranean world. "Thou art, and thou alone, all the goddesses which different people call by different names," went an old hymn. Unlike many Egyptian deities, Isis was not depicted as an animal but had her own beautiful face and

figure. This may partly account for her wide appeal to so many nations. But her greatest appeal was her reputation for love and compassion, her ability to forgive and to heal. And her role as champion of women and children made her the ideal goddess for women everywhere.

With the magic of her title, the New Isis, Cleopatra seemed less of an outsider, more acceptable to her Egyptian subjects. Whether her identity with Isis was mostly political propaganda or not, it was winning her subjects' loyalty.

Immersed in her role as goddess-queen and mother, Cleopatra was also waiting impatiently for a summons from Caesar to visit him in Rome.

Isis nursing her baby son, often identified with Cleopatra nursing her baby, Caesarion.

FOUR

∿∿∿∿∿∿∿∿∿∿∿∿∿

CAESAR THE DICTATOR

❧

. . . he doth bestride the narrow world
Like a Colossus . . .
—SHAKESPEARE'S *JULIUS CAESAR,*
ACT I, SCENE II

On his way back to Rome, Caesar had to deal with a rebellion that had broken out in northern Asia Minor. He suppressed the rebels so swiftly that he wrote to a friend, "Veni, vidi, vici,"—"I came, I saw, I conquered." He was now almost at the pinnacle of his power and could look forward to fulfilling his dream of being a second Alexander the Great. In fact, Caesar's megalomania was beginning to show.

In spite of having put his trusted friend Mark Antony in charge of his interests in Rome while he pursued Pompey to Egypt, Caesar found considerable unrest upon his return. His legions were on the verge of mutiny, demanding pay and land. Enriched by his stay in the east, Caesar promised them both pay and land, and after a rousing speech, his soldiers were ready to die for him. Then in a magnanimous gesture he pardoned Pompey's soldiers who had fought against him the year before. His popularity with the Roman populace soared, though there were still many conservative republicans, whose opposition to his power was growing stronger every day. Despite this, Caesar was named Dictator, a temporary official position designed to deal with a crisis. When the crisis ended, he was expected to step down. As Dictator, Caesar had complete authority over the entire Roman government.

The civil war was not over yet. Pompey's sons, eager to avenge their father's death, were still at large, gathering republican forces to oppose Caesar in the Roman province of North Africa. So once again he was off to battle, and once again he routed his Roman political enemies. The proud and honest republican senator Cato committed suicide rather than submit to a dictator who, he feared, aimed to be dictator for life.

In fact, the battle in North Africa and Cato's death seemed to some to spell the end of the Roman Republic. Caesar had come to scorn the Republic as outdated and nothing but a name "without form or substance." Even the great orator Cicero, who would do everything in his power to save the Republic, knew how far it had declined. A great historian, Mommsen, wrote: "In Rome men had forgotten what honesty was." Many of the once highly respected senators now thought more of keeping their wealth and privileges than restoring good government. Cicero scornfully reproached such selfish senators, saying, "Those fools think more of saving their fishponds than the Republic." Caesar, on the other hand, saw no sense in keeping the Republic and felt the future of Rome, with its new overseas provinces, lay in one-man rule, and he was more and more certain that he was the man for that role.

Back in Rome at the end of summer 46 B.C., Caesar began preparations for four separate triumphs, the Roman versions of victory parades, commemorating his victories in Gaul, Egypt, Asia Minor, and North Africa.

Caesar's triumphs were the most elaborate pageants ever seen in Rome and surely were inspired by the sumptuous extravaganzas he had witnessed in Alexandria. They lasted four days, one day for each of his victories, though Caesar was careful to omit celebrating his defeat of the popular Pompey, with whom so many fellow Romans had been killed. He did, however, make the mistake of celebrating his North African victory, after which Cato had killed himself. Cato had become a symbol of honest republican government and had grown more powerful in death than in life. He was the inspiration to return to normal, constitutional government, the balanced rule of the senate and the people of Rome.

In the triumphal parade celebrating his victory in Alexandria, one float represented the great Pharos lighthouse with artificial flames shooting out at the top and huge placards depicting the deaths of the eunuch Pothinus and the Alexandrian army commander. Then came a float with the spoils of war, the vast treasure of gold and silver, jewels and objects of art, that Caesar had helped himself to in his eastern conquests. The climax was a parade of distinguished prisoners, among whom was Cleopatra's young half-sister, Arsinoë, weighted down in chains. This was not popular with the Roman crowd, who felt a twinge of compassion at the sight of such a young girl as a prisoner of war. At least Caesar didn't put her to death, as he did other prominent prisoners.

Winding up each day's procession was Caesar himself. Dressed in a purple robe trimmed with gold stars, he stood erect in a gilded chariot drawn by white horses. The heavy gold crown of the Roman god Jupiter was held over his head. In contrast to this regal pomp, the soldiers' bawdy songs could be heard above the martial music—"Home we bring our bald-headed lecher/Romans, lock your wives away."

After these great spectacles Caesar distributed some of his looted treasure to his soldiers and gave a costly feast for Rome's citizens. It required 22,000 couches, on each of which reclined three diners. Then came weeks of games, for which Caesar provided a novelty of silk awnings (an eastern luxury) to shield people from the sun. Comfortable beneath the awnings, the people watched gladiatorial shows in which prisoners of war were pitted against condemned criminals in deadly combat. Exciting and equally brutal wild-beast shows followed, with hunters shooting arrows or hurling spears at bewildered animals from North Africa—lions, elephants, and giraffes (never before seen in Rome). The final extravaganza was a mock sea battle in an artificial lake, built especially for the occasion.

With all this lavish entertainment, the free food and wine, the people went wild with enthusiasm for their great military hero. They were ready to give him anything he asked for. In fact, Roman adulation of military leaders had been mounting for many years; whoever controlled an army could now control the civil government. The populace, as well as the soldiers, felt more allegiance to a military leader than to Rome's once prestigious senate.

Cleopatra had finally received her summons from Caesar to visit him in Rome. Soon after the military celebrations, in the fall of 46 B.C. , she arrived with her co-ruler brother and her baby son, Caesarion. It was Cleopatra and their son whom Caesar wished to see, not her brother. But it would have been risky to leave him behind, lest he start some palace intrigue to gain the throne in the Queen's absence. Caesar had invited Cleopatra to come as a state visitor, an independent queen, an ally of Rome. She brought a huge retinue, her bodyguard of eunuchs, her courtiers, a philosopher friend, the astronomer Sosigenes, and a prominent musician, as well as many servants. They were housed in Caesar's villa, surrounded by spacious gardens near the Tiber River. Reports of feasting, music, and merriment in the villa were greeted with raised eyebrows by the establishment, those moralstic conservative Romans. Not all, however, felt this way—Caesar's close friend Mark Antony highly enjoyed the dining and wining and especially Cleopatra's lively company. He had not forgotten meeting her as a teenager when he had been in Alexandria to help her father.

By and large, this visit of a foreign queen, a detested easterner, Caesar's mistress—along with their illegitimate son—caused a sensation. No one knows what Caesar's wife, Calpurnia, thought of it, but she was well used to Caesar's womanizing; her marriage to Caesar had been purely political, as were his two earlier ones and most marriages among Roman politicians. Caesar made no effort to conceal his attachment to Cleopatra and was unconcerned at the scandal it caused. Both he and Cleopatra had no trouble in disregarding society's conventions when it suited them.

But when Caesar opened his new temple dedicated to the Roman goddess Venus, the Romans were in for a real shock. Standing next to Venus's statue stood a golden one of Cleopatra! This might be a great honor and compliment to Egypt's Queen, but it was deeply offensive to the Romans to have their revered goddess next to a foreigner, whether a queen or goddess, or both. Was Caesar suggesting that Cleopatra, the New Isis, equaled the Roman goddess Venus? In fact, Isis, by this time, was identical with Venus and Aphrodite, the same goddess under three different names. Since Caesar liked to boast that he was descended from Venus, he seemed to imply that he and Cleopatra-Isis were divinely connected.

In any case, Caesar's bold gesture did imply that his relationship with Cleopatra was more than just a casual love affair. Was it something more serious? People began to worry that Caesar was thinking of marrying her, and

Greek sculptured head of Cleopatra, thought to be authentic but may be more an imitation of her style than a real likeness.

that his stay in Egypt, where divine god-rulers had complete authority, had indeed affected him. Was he aiming to be a god-ruler too?

How much Cleopatra influenced Caesar in his thoughts of one-man rule is not known, but in their joint ambition to rule the Mediterranean world, she likely egged him on to thoughts of monarchy. She must have been pleased at his dictatorship, his not having to pay attention to those republican senators arguing over laws and affairs of state. Like Caesar, she had little use for the concepts of the Roman Republic, so foreign to her way of running a government. And, as dictator, Caesar had the power to pass any law he wished. Cleopatra was grateful to have him dictate to the Senate a treaty confirming her status as Queen of Egypt, a friend and ally of Rome. She would not have to worry anymore that Rome might annex Egypt as a province.

However much Cleopatra led Caesar toward his imperial aims, her influence on him in other ways was beneficial. It was at this time that the astronomer Sosigenes helped Caesar reform the calendar so that it agreed with the seasons. It became known as the Julian calendar, and is essentially the one we use today. Caesar also planned to build canals like the ones he had seen in Alexandria and to drain marshes. Impressed by Alexandria's great library, he started to build several public ones in Rome.

Caesar had to interrupt his busy life for one last battle with Pompey's sons, who had escaped to Spain and were stirring up a rebellion. Victorious again, Caesar was made dictator for life upon his return.

And now he buckled down to a project he had long contemplated, his most ambitious military venture of all—the conquest of Parthia, the menacing empire east of Syria. Thoughts of greater glory, of being a second Alexander the Great, of extending Rome's empire all the way to India, consumed him. He would retrieve Rome's honor and wipe out the stain of Parthia's humiliating defeat of Roman legions nine years earlier. Rome could never accept defeat without revenge. Caesar likely discussed his plans with Cleopatra, who was eager to help him and, at the same time, regain Egypt's lost territories. She envisioned sharing leadership with him.

But Caesar didn't seem to realize the fear and anger that were building up among the staunch old republicans. Cicero clearly saw the handwriting on the wall, an end to his beloved Republic. Would the clock be turned back five hundred years, to a hated monarchy? Already Caesar had allowed his statue to be erected alongside the seven early kings of Rome and was given the privilege of wearing the purple garb and high red boots of ancient kings. At one time his statue was paraded alongside statues of the Roman gods and goddesses. Was the populace aiming to deify him? Cicero thought that Cleopatra was partly to blame for all this adulation of Caesar and wished the Queen would go back to Alexandria.

Added to the gossip that Caesar planned to marry Cleopatra (to marry a foreigner was taboo in Rome) and move the capital from Rome to Alexandria came a startling and upsetting rumor. The sacred Sibylline Books, Rome's own collection of oracles, consulted in times of crisis and often used for political propaganda, had prophesied that only a king could defeat the Parthians. It was said that at the next senate meeting Caesar would have himself proclaimed King! The very word *king* was hateful to Romans of all classes.

Caesar's good friend Mark Antony had placed a crown on Caesar's head during a Roman festival. When

Caesar removed it, saying, "I am not King but Caesar," wild applause had broken out. Still, a shiver of fear ran through the crowd. Had Caesar arranged this stunt to test the people's desire to make him King, or to show he would never take the title? No one knows the answer— some have thought he wanted to be called King only during his forthcoming campaign in the East, knowing he could never get away with it in Rome. On the other hand, he didn't seem to care or fear what people thought. Of course, he had no need for kingship. As dictator for life, he already had all the power of a king. But to Romans the title *king* had long meant a despotic tyrant, whereas a dictator was appointed by the government for a period of time. And though Caesar was dictator for life, he could not legally pass on his title to an heir, as a king could. Kingship would mean the cold reality of the end of the Republic. The old guard of conservative senators, resenting Caesar's power, his arrogance, and his scorn of their opinions, were now deeply worried that the dictator was indeed becoming a tyrant.

Caesar was impatient to be off with his devoted soldiers on his last big military enterprise, to get away from the petty criticism and the stifling atmosphere of Rome. With a new victory and with Cleopatra and her vast wealth, he would, like Alexander the Great, be a world ruler, with the power to award himself any title he might choose.

It was in the late winter of 44 B.C., not long before the senate was to meet on the ides (or fifteenth) of March, that a conspiracy began to form behind closed doors. "Tyranny must end, Caesar must die," was whispered among the sixty conspirators. They were mostly of the senatorial class, some close friends of Caesar, some whom he had pardoned even though they had fought against him. They called themselves liberators and planned to assassinate the "tyrant" at the forthcoming senate meeting. Caesar's own plan was to leave for his eastern campaign just two days after the meeting.

The two ringleaders of the conspiracy were Cassius, who hated Caesar for personal reasons, and Brutus, an honorable, respected republican, related to Cato and a descendant of another Brutus, the famous hero who had driven out Rome's last king five hundred years before and helped set up Rome's Republic. Brutus lent dignity and hope to the conspiracy.

A kind of unease pervaded the city, and Caesar may have suspected some sort of plot, but he showed no outward fear. He had even given up his bodyguard after obtaining an oath of loyalty from all Roman citizens. When warned of evil omens, he arrogantly replied that omens would be as he wished. While dining with friends the night before the senate meeting, he was asked what kind of death he would choose. "Let it come swiftly," answered Caesar.

The next morning, as he was walking up the steps to the senate assembly, someone handed him a note of warning, but Caesar didn't bother to read it. When he was seated inside, one of the conspirators approached him as though to beg a favor. Caesar tried to brush him aside, but instead the conspirator stepped closer and yanked at Caesar's toga, baring his shoulder. This was the signal to the other conspirators who now rushed on him with their daggers drawn. He soon slumped to the ground and lay in a pool of blood, pierced by twenty-three wounds. In one hand lay the unread note of warning.

So great Caesar perished, but the expected cry of liberty and freedom did not ring out from the masses. Instead, people panicked and locked themselves in their houses. Even the liberators' exultation turned to fear, as confusion and chaos spread through the terror-stricken city. The assassins soon had to worry about saving their own skins when Caesar's veteran soldiers, shattered by the death of their great leader, rose in anger for revenge.

A few day later Antony gave a rousing funeral speech in the Roman Forum before a huge crowd. He reminded the people of Caesar's great exploits, and of his clemency even to his enemies. Then he read aloud part of Caesar's will and revealed the dictator's generous bequests of money and land to the people of Rome. In a final dramatic flourish, he held up Caesar's bloody toga for all to see. Pandemonium broke loose. The fickle crowd, who would have refused the dictator a kingly crown, now joined the soldiers in shouting and yelling for vengeance. Antony's eloquence had changed the image of Caesar from tyrant to martyr.

In Caesar's villa across the Tiber River, Queen Cleopatra was devastated at the news of his murder. She had lost her lover, the father of her son, and her protector. All her hopes were dashed, the future murky and uncertain. As soon as she could, she set sail for Egypt.

Caesar's assassination on the ides of March.

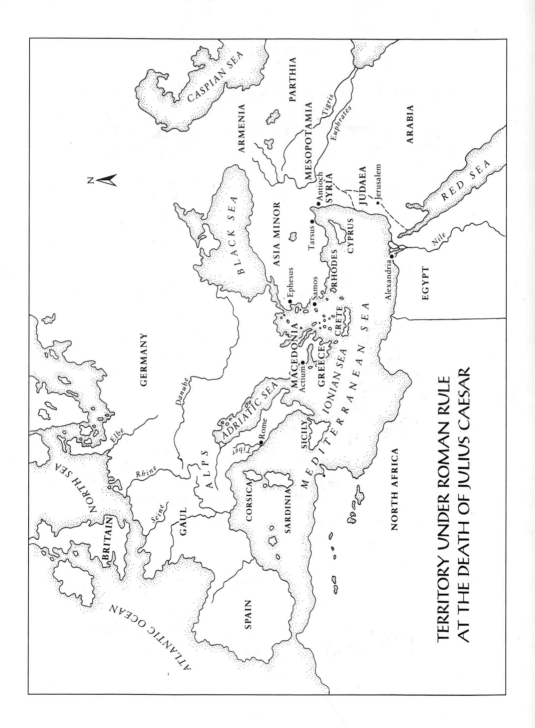

Map of Roman territories.

FIVE

~~~~~~~~~~~~~~~~~~~

ANTONY AND CLEOPATRA

And then the whole wide world
under a Woman's hand
ruled and obeying everywhere shall stand,
the Widow shall queen the whole wide world.
—SIBYLLINE ORACLE

Back in Alexandria, Cleopatra was faced with a sea of troubles, but she was as determined as ever to keep her power.

Shortly after their return, her brother, Ptolemy XIV, mysteriously died, perhaps poisoned at Cleopatra's orders. There is no clear evidence of this, only suspicion that she wanted him out of the way so that her little son, Caesarion, would be the only legitimate heir to the throne.

Then, as had happened earlier in her reign, the Nile

once more failed in its annual flooding, and the growing season was so bad that famine set in. Some of the starving people even sold themselves into slavery in order to be fed. To alleviate the situation, Cleopatra opened reserve granaries in Alexandria and distributed grain to the populace. She also forbade tax gatherers, noted for gouging the poor, to collect anything beyond the minimum tax on land.

Cleopatra ruled alone for the next three years, a time of peace with no uprisings in her country. And she made the most of her role as the New Isis and was revered almost as a savior by her subjects. She was also thought of as the widow of her divine husband Caesar, and Caesarion was recognized as their divine offspring.

Cleopatra was determined, at all costs, to keep Egypt's independence and try to regain its lost overseas possessions: Cyprus, Syria, Judaea, Palestine, and Lebanon. But she knew she needed some strong military man to take Julius Caesar's place, a new consort to stand by her lest Rome once more try to grab her kingdom. She listened eagerly to any news from Rome brought by sailors or merchants; she even sent scouts there to gather information.

But the confusing reports from Rome, where events and alliances were changing daily, only added to her worries. Who would be in charge now that Caesar was gone? What Roman should she try to deal with? Had she lost all her prestige with Caesar's friends? Could she count on Caesar's devoted friend Mark Antony to help her? Did Caesar's decree that she was Queen of Egypt, ally and friend of Rome, still hold? Or was she, once again, a mere client queen whom they could boss around? Such questions pressed on her continually.

Her great hope, that little Caesarion would be recognized as Caesar's son and heir as well as the future King of Egypt, had already been challenged. Caesar's will made no mention of him and, much to Cleopatra's dismay, named his great-nephew, nineteen-year-old Octavius, as his adopted son and heir. (Though never proved, there was a rumor that Caesar had made a second will naming Caesarion his heir, which he had planned to announce upon being made King on the ides of March.) It must have infuriated Cleopatra to learn that Octavius was calling himself Caesar. Further, the Romans who had not allowed Julius Caesar to be King while he lived, declared him a god soon after his assassination. The appearance of a bright comet in the sky confirmed that Caesar's soul had risen to join the immortal gods dwelling in the heavens. So Octavius could now claim that he was the son of a god. Cleopatra naturally felt that her son had prior claim to Caesar's name and divinity, since he was the only known surviving child of his blood.

Mark Antony was equally put out by Octavius and scoffed at the young man "who owes everything to a name." Antony felt that he, Caesar's old military companion and favored friend, should take the dictator's place. He was well known and popular, especially with the army men, who adored him as they had Caesar for his expert military leadership as well as for his good companionship. But he underestimated Caesar's young

nephew, who was having great political success because
of the famous name he had inherited and who was just
as ambitious as Antony and far more clever and calculat-
ing. There was little love between them, but they both realized they should band together to bring order to their
chaotic country and prepare to pursue the conspirators.
Led by Brutus and Cassius, Caesar's republican enemies
had fled to Greece. In their absence, Antony, Octavius,
and a third friend of Caesar, Lepidus, formed a second
Triumvirate. Unlike Caesar, who had shown clemency to
his enemies, they indulged in a ruthless massacre, an
orgy of killing all who opposed them, even those merely
suspected of doing so.

One victim was the orator Cicero, needlessly murdered
for his bitter attacks on Antony, whose close ties with
the Dictator Caesar he had long resented and whose
debauchery and licentious living he despised. Cicero's
fiery words could often make or break a politician. Upon
seeing the orator's severed head, Antony's brutal wife,
Fulvia, thrust a pin through the tongue that had spoken
against her husband, as though she feared this famous
tongue had a life of its own.

After the bloodthirsty reign of terror and after collecting the wealth and land of the murdered men, the three
new leaders set off in pursuit of the main enemy conspirators.

When Cleopatra realized that another civil war between Romans was imminent, she started to build a fleet
to prepare for the coming struggle. She knew she would
be pressured by both sides to give aid in money, ships,

Mark Antony, whose powerful build and curly hair made him so resemble Hercules.

and grain. However, she decided to take her time in deciding which side to support—Egypt's and her own future depended on her choosing the winner. It was a dilemma for her—she knew and liked Antony but mistrusted Octavius, whom she did not know. Yet she could hardly have wanted to join with Cassius or Brutus and the other assassins of her dead lover, even though they were already badgering her for help.

Then Cleopatra got news that Antony and Octavius had agreed to recognize her son. Could she trust this rumor? If so, they would be the better bet. Octavius was probably persuaded by Antony to go along with this agreement only because he was eager to lay hands on Cleopatra's famed wealth and supplies. He inwardly feared her and her son as threats to his future. It was Octavius who later would use every kind of propaganda to smear Cleopatra as the vile and monstrous "serpent of the Nile."

Cleopatra was soon at sea commanding her fleet, the only woman to do so since a Greek warrior queen, Artemesia, had commanded a navy in battle centuries earlier. Cleopatra headed northwest to join Antony and Octavius's fleet, which had just left Italy. But she didn't get far before a violent storm wrecked many of her ships and she fell ill. She returned to Alexandria with little accomplished except an impressive show of courage.

Luckily for the Queen, the triumvirs quickly triumphed over the conspirators, whose leaders, Brutus and Cassius, committed suicide upon defeat. So ended the "liberators" and their cause of freedom from tyranny. The last breath of republicanism was extinguished—henceforth Rome would boast an Empire, to be ruled by the new Triumvirate.

Octavius went back to Italy to take charge of the West, and Antony, who had served in Syria and been to Egypt to help restore Cleopatra's father, happily stayed in the wealthy East. The third and somewhat insignificant triumvir, Lepidus, was allotted a smaller portion of Roman provinces.

The next contact that Cleopatra had with the Romans was a summons from Antony, who had settled in the town of Tarsus on the coast of what is now southern Turkey. He was glorying in his victory over Brutus and Cassius. And well he might, for it was largely his military skill that had won the day. Octavius had fallen ill and been unable to fight. Antony felt confident that he would be recognized as the number-one leader of the Roman Empire. Like Alexander the Great, he was hailed as the New Dionysus, the title Cleopatra's father had assumed with so little success. But unlike her father, Antony was a conquering hero and, the people hoped, a bringer of peace.

God-rulers had become a dime a dozen in the eastern Mediterranean world. Divine titles gave rulers prestige and authority and gave the people a chance to express their hero worship. Though Antony had often posed as Hercules, he happily shifted to Dionysus, now the most popular god in the East. He was greatly flattered by the title of divinity and felt it showed that the people trusted him to save them from their enemies and give them hope for a better life. Dionysus had become *the* savior god even as Isis was *the* savior goddess.

Cleopatra did not answer Antony's first summons, nor the second, nor the third. Her immediate reaction was, Why should she go to him? Better that he should come to her. But finally, knowing that Egypt's fate depended on which Roman commanded the East, she accepted. Still, she took her time, time she needed to prepare a spectacular arrival and to use all her womanly arts to impress and captivate the New Dionysus. She was not going rolled up in a carpet this time but in her royal golden barge, a barge fit for a goddess-queen.

As Cleopatra set off and watched the sails of purple silk billowing in the wind, words of a hymn to Isis may have run through her mind: "I am Isis . . . I am the Queen of rivers and winds and the sea." The oars were made of silver, and they dipped in time to the musical beat of flutes, fifes, and harps. Cleopatra, dressed as Aphrodite-Isis, reclined under a canopy of gold cloth. Beautiful young boys, like painted cupids, stood by her side to cool her with fans. Her maids-in-waiting were dressed like sea nymphs, some steering at the rudder, others working at the ropes.

The town of Tarsus lay on the banks of the river Cyndus, and as the barge sailed upriver, multitudes swarmed to the river's edge to gaze in wonder at the sight, enhanced by the delicious scent of perfumes wafting to the shore. Word spread that "Aphrodite had come to revel with Dionysus for the happiness of Asia." Cleopatra's skillful

Statuette of Isis as protecting spirit, from the tomb of Tutankhamen.

showmanship was also clever propaganda—to show the people that two divinities were coming together to rule over them. Whether she was called Aphrodite, Venus or Isis, whether Antony was called Dionysus or Osiris, didn't matter, since the titles were now interchangeable.

Cleopatra knew Antony well enough to know how much he would enjoy her luxurious spectacle, and she was hopeful that he would soon take Caesar's place as her protecter and promoter. Not only would Egypt be hers, but the whole Mediterranean world would be ruled under their joint partnership.

At first Antony had stayed aloof, expecting Cleopatra to come ashore to dine with him. She refused. Instead, she asked him to dine with her aboard her royal barge. She won, and Antony came to her. At home on the battle-field or off carousing with actors and actresses, the unsophisticated Antony was dazzled by the exquisite taste of the Queen who had used every art to captivate him—the best craftsmen and the best entertainers of Alexandria, to say nothing of the most exotic foods cooked to perfection. Small lighted lanterns hung from tree branches suspended overhead, turning the scene into an enchanted garden. When they sat down to the sumptuous feast, beautiful dancers and musicians provided entertainment.

A few days later Antony managed to lure the Queen to dine at his home, and though he used much of his wealth to make the dinner a success, it couldn't compare with Cleopatra's display. Antony luckily had a sense of humor. He could laugh at himself and joked about his inadequacy as a host.

Antony was always susceptible to alluring women, and he and Cleopatra soon became lovers as well as political partners, knowing that they could help each other—Cleopatra with her fabulous wealth and political acumen, Antony with his military ability, fame, and pop-ularity. Though Antony was married to Fulvia, his domineering third wife, marital fidelity didn't constrain him any more than it had Caesar. But it was pretty heady stuff and quite overwhelming for the rather naive and unsophisticated Antony to have a queen as his mistress.

The couple's first business was to make sure that there were no rivals to their power. Cleopatra's young sister, Arsinoë, who had been paraded in Caesar's Roman triumph, had taken refuge not far from Tarsus and, for the second time, was accused of plotting to usurp Cleopatra's throne. She was already being hailed Queen of Egypt by her followers. Cleopatra would not stand any more sibling rivalry for her throne. At her request, Antony had Arsinoë put to death for treason. Now there was no one left in the royal family to challenge her. The only other Ptolemy was her little son, Caesarion, whom she adored and planned to make her successor.

When Cleopatra returned to Alexandria, Antony pub-licly confirmed Cleopatra's right to the throne of Egypt and stayed behind to check up on the loyalty of various kingdoms in the East. He was preparing the region to carry out Caesar's projected war on Parthia. Then he fol-lowed the Queen, to spend the winter of 41–40 B.C. as her guest in Alexandria. Remembering Caesar's unwelcome entry to the city, Antony came as a private citizen, unaccompanied by soldiers.

Cleopatra was now twenty-eight years old, a woman's most glamorous and appealing age, according to some. Antony was forty-five, still youthful-looking and full of vitality (unlike his bald-headed friend Caesar, he had a mass of curly hair). Cleopatra found him attractive and full of fun, if not as interesting intellectually as Caesar.

Their relationship at first was based on their need for each other in the political world. But they also came to depend on each other more and more, perhaps not as passionately as Shakespeare suggested in his play *Antony and Cleopatra*, but with deepening affection. Cleopatra may have had the upper hand in their relationship, but despite some disagreements, she remained faithful to Antony just as she had been to Caesar. She was never promiscuous, as her enemies suggested—such behavior was beneath her queenly dignity. If she had ever had any other lovers, her enemies surely would have found out and made the most of it. None were ever mentioned. Ptolemy queens might be murderous, but they were not adulterous.

With the charismatic Antony now at her side, Cleopatra did everything she could to keep him entertained. Antony, like Caesar, found Cleopatra not only the perfect mistress but also a perfect companion. She even indulged his tastes, which were considerably cruder than hers—his love of feasting, drinking, gambling, and bawdy jokes. They gathered around them a band of Alexandria's gilded youth and called themselves "The Inimitable Livers"—

those who live life to the full. Exaggerated tales that they painted the town red in drunken debauchery made good gossip in Rome. Certainly Antony, always something of a playboy, enjoyed drinking, but Cleopatra never had any such reputation until her enemies spread the word that she was continually steeped in wine.

It is now thought that the Inimitable Livers may have been a group of initiates in the religious rites of Dionysus. The Roman accusation that Cleopatra drank too much was probably their misunderstanding of a sacred ring she wore in connection with these rites. The ring held an amethyst, symbol of sobriety, but on the amethyst was engraved a tiny goddess of drunkenness, to signify "sober drunkenness." This odd contradiction embodied the idea that one could get drunk without drinking. Women in the Dionysian revels often got "drunk" without liquor, from dancing themselves into a state of frenzy or spiritual ecstasy, like the whirling dervishes of later times. Romans couldn't understand this and didn't approve of dancing anyway—they didn't think anyone could dance without drinking. In fact, the practical Romans didn't understand the appeal of any of the mystical and emotional religions so popular in the East; they tried to ban them in Italy.

Cleopatra was also criticized for her reckless extravagance. The Romans circulated a tale of her trying to impress Antony with her wealth. At one of their feasts, so the tale went, she removed a huge pearl of great value from her earring, dissolved it in a cup of vinegar, and swallowed it! Vinegar does not dissolve pearls, and any

Girl dancing in a Dionysian festival. Note her head thrown back as she begins to twirl into an ecstasy.

∿∿∿∿∿∿∿∿∿∿∿∿∿∿∿∿∿∿∿∿∿∿∿∿∿∿∿∿∿

acid strong enough to do so would have killed her. So much for Roman stories to blacken the Queen.

But Cleopatra did go to great lengths to entertain and amuse Antony, even joining him on hunting and fishing trips. One amusing fish story might have a basis in truth. Accompanied by Cleopatra, Antony was embarrassed by having no luck catching fish, not even a nibble, so he secretly got a message to some fishermen to dive underwater and attach fish already caught to his hook. Then he happily began pulling in fish after fish. It didn't take Cleopatra long to discover the trick, but she pretended to admire his skill. Telling friends of the episode, she invited them to join her and Antony the next day. Before Antony dropped his line from the boat, she sent down a diver with a salted fish to attach to his hook. When Antony pulled in his catch, all burst out laughing at the sight of the long-dead fish. "Leave your fishing rod to us poor rulers in Alexandria; your game is provinces and kingdoms," advised the Queen, perhaps suggesting he should get going on the more important projects he had planned.

Apart from such silly escapades, Cleopatra was able to interest Antony in the visual arts and in conversing with learned men of letters and philosophy. Antony, an admirer of all things Greek, was impressed with Cleopatra's wide literary knowledge. Later he presented the Queen with an entire collection of scrolls from another eastern city that had boasted a library almost equal to Alexandria's. This gift helped make up for the scrolls lost in the fire during Caesar's battle in the harbor.

Antony had planned to leave Egypt in the spring to prepare for his attack on Parthia, but he left sooner than expected upon hearing disturbing news. The Parthians had gotten the jump on him and were themselves attacking Syria; several neighboring kings already had defected to the enemy. Antony left immediately, only to be confronted with further bad news when he reached Syria—his wife, Fulvia, and his brother, without consulting him, had started an uprising against Octavius and had been utterly defeated.

Once again Cleopatra was abandoned by her consort, and once again she was pregnant. In the fall of 40 B.C. she gave birth to twins, a boy and a girl. She named the boy Alexander, after Alexander the Great, the legendary founder of her royal dynasty. She knew this would please Antony, who was counting on being a second Alexander once he had defeated Parthia. She gave the girl her own auspicious name, Cleopatra. Names were all-important to royalty, and the Queen's choices showed she still had hope of future glory for herself, her family, and her kingdom of Egypt. Already oracles were chanting her glory to the world.

Oracles or prophecies often expressed people's longings, and at this time there was widespread longing for peace, an end to Roman conquest in the East, an end to the Parthian menace. Many of these oracles pointed to Cleopatra, the New Isis, as the one who would save them:

There comes a woman's great power . . .
when royal dignity and crown she takes . . .
Earth will be free for all, unwalled, unfenced. . . .

Such lofty hopes were circulating all over the East.

SIX

〰〰〰〰〰〰〰〰〰〰〰〰〰

ANTONY ABANDONS CLEOPATRA

And from the vault of Heaven above,
a newborn child comes down. . . .
He'll rule the peaceful earth.
—VIRGIL, FOURTH ECLOGUE

Cleopatra would not see Antony for the next three and a half years, but she was kept well informed about his doings, none of which were comforting. The Queen's astrologer had accompanied Antony and not only reported news to her but also acted on her behalf in trying to persuade Antony not to trust Octavius.

Despite the longing for peace, so evident in poetry and oracles, war loomed ever closer. For Antony, preparing to check the Parthian invasion of Syria, the news of his wife's failed revolt against Octavius seemed a catastrophe.

He decided he must go back to Italy right away. He had no desire to break with Octavius at this point—he desperately needed his cooperation if he was to successfully recruit Roman legions in Italy. He was angry at his wife, Fulvia, for starting the rebellion without even consulting him, and he worried that she might have damaged his future. He soon learned that his wife, unhappy at his angry reaction to her attempts to help him, had fallen ill and died.

Antony expected to meet Octavius at the seaport of Brundiseum, but there was no sign of his partner, and the gates of the city were closed against him. Despite many faults, Antony always respected agreements and trusted Octavius to do the same. He was annoyed, and grew more so when he learned that his partner had not lived up to their agreement to share Italy equally for recruiting and quartering soldiers. In fact, Octavius had taken more than his share of land for his own men and was increasing his legions at the expense of Antony's.

Eventually the two partners met in an atmosphere of tension. Soon it looked as if another civil war would break out, this time between the two triumvirs—they still called themselves triumvirs, though the third one, Lepidus, was more and more ignored. Luckily the soldiers themselves didn't have the heart for another war of Romans fighting Romans. Finally, in the fall of 40 B.C., a new pact of peace was made, using marriage contracts to cement it. (Roman women were often used as pawns in political deals. To abandon one wife for a more politically useful one was easily arranged—by the men, of course.) Octavius divorced his wife and married another man's wife of the old republican faction in order to gain support from that group—still important though considerably shrunken after the massacre. Within a year he would discard her for another married woman of even more political clout.

For his part Antony agreed to marry Octavius's beautiful and virtuous sister, Octavia. It was hoped that this marriage would bolster friendly relations between the two co-rulers. The war-weary Romans rejoiced, thinking a new era of peace had come at last. The poet Virgil wrote a poem to celebrate the marriage, prophesying that the couple would have a son to usher in an age of peace and prosperity.

Octavia did soon have a baby, but it turned out to be a girl, not the hoped-for "prince of peace." Cleopatra did not rejoice at hearing that it was Antony's new marriage that had reestablished peace between the triumvirs. It was a blow not only to her pride but also to her plans. And that Octavia was young, beautiful, and virtuous was not exactly welcome news. But Cleopatra was not one to despair, and she was very busy as a mother and Queen.

It may have been at this time that some of the practical and learned books attributed to Cleopatra appeared—one on weights, measures, and coins, another on medicine and gynecology, one on alchemy, and last, perhaps least, one on cosmetics. In this a cure prescribed for baldness does not sound like the learned Queen's handiwork: "Of domestic mice, burnt, 1 part; . . . of horse's teeth, burnt, 1 part; of bear's grease, 1 part; of deer marrow, 1 part; of reed-bark, 1 part. To be pounded when dry and mixed with lots of honey; and the bald part rubbed (with this mixture) till it sprouts"! It was more likely a work commissioned by the Queen than written by her. Whether the cure for baldness was inspired by Caesar's lack of hair is not known. Cleopatra herself would have been more interested in the mixtures of plants, seaweeds, and mulberry juices prescribed for different tints of rouge.

Not long after Antony went back to Rome, the Queen had a visit from a handsome, clever young man named Herod (later famed as Herod the Great, King of the Jews.) He was terribly upset at the fate of his little country, Judaea, which the Parthians had invaded along with Syria. Left by Antony in charge of the area, Herod had been unable to stave off the enemy and had barely managed to escape alive. Knowing the Queen's attachment to Antony, he came to Alexandria seeking her help. Cleopatra could not forget that Judaea had once belonged to her family. Nevertheless she received him cordially and listened to his tale of woe. She gave him a ship to sail to Italy, where he hoped to get Antony's military help to save his country. Cleopatra did this to please Antony, who she knew needed dedicated leaders to combat the Parthians. Herod was more successful than he dared hope. Both Antony and Octavius, seeing in this ambitious young man an ally who would be useful, agreed to make him King of Judaea. Neither the Queen nor Herod suspected then that she and he would later become bitter enemies.

The next disconcerting news to reach Cleopatra was that Antony and his wife Octavia—and their new baby girl—were living in Athens while she was tending Antony's twins alone in Alexandria. It must have hurt deeply to learn that the new couple were hailed as Aphrodite and Dionysus, just as she and Antony had been a few years before.

Though Antony was apparently enjoying life with his lovely young wife, he was not neglecting plans for his great campaign against Parthia. Before he attacked Parthia itself, he directed his generals to clear the way by pushing the enemy out of the lands Parthia had just conquered—Syria and surrounding areas. Herod was helpful in retaking Judaea, and Antony's best Roman general managed to recapture land as far as the Euphrates River, beyond which lay Parthia itself. A powerful Parthian prince was killed, and Antony himself dashed east to help his general finish off a resistant city on the Euphrates. There was great rejoicing among both Greeks and Romans. It looked as though the Parthian menace might soon end, that Rome's earlier defeat could be fully avenged. Antony's star was in the ascendancy.

Outwardly Octavius backed the enthusiasm for Antony's success, but inwardly he was jealous, especially since he was not doing well dealing with the last of Pompey's sons, who had become a renegade Roman outlaw known as the "Sea King" and who had grabbed some of Rome's islands and was menacing Italy itself.

In 38 B.C., Octavius called Antony back to Italy to

help deal with this troublesome pirate—or so he said. More likely Octavius was eager to interrupt and delay Antony's successes.

Antony dutifully came back, only to find that Octavius had double-crossed him again and had failed to show up. No one had warned Antony that Octavius, postponing his problem with the Sea King, was now in the north gaining military glory against some barbarian tribes. Antony, miffed at this snub and eager to get on with his eastern campaign, went right back to Athens. (Going right back was a matter of several weeks' sailing.)

He was angry and upset. Henceforth relations between him and Octavius became more and more strained. Perhaps Antony now remembered Cleopatra's warning not to trust his co-ruler. For the moment, however, Octavia managed to smooth things over between husband and brother, though her patching of their differences always seemed to end in her brother's favor.

Octavius and his skillful commander had achieved great military glory in the north, but Rome was still being harassed by the Sea King. In 37 B.C., Octavius, sounding desperate, sent still another summons to Antony asking for more ships. It was probably due to Octavia's persuasion that her husband agreed to go back once more to Italy. His wife accompanied him, and they were followed by a fleet of three hundred ships.

Once again Octavius wasn't there to meet Antony. This time Antony, though complaining bitterly of his fleet lying idle and his partner's repeated failures to keep his word, decided to wait. He would use the time to check up on his own political standing with the Romans and to recruit much-needed soldiers. He and Octavius finally met and signed still another peace pact, which renewed their partnership for another five years.

But on his way back to Athens, Antony began to brood over his co-ruler's insulting treatment, his repeated broken promises. He had given Octavius ships but as yet had not been given the legions promised in return. Even worse, he had lost a year's preparation for his campaign by all these unnecessary trips to Italy.

Antony's gradual disillusionment with and distrust of Octavius finally burst out—he felt he could stand it no longer. When they put in at an island, he sent Octavia, who was pregnant with another child, back to Italy, explaining that he must hurry east to finish off his war against Parthia. A great victory in the East was his only hope to compete with Octavius's growing power in the West. He realized now that their partnership was hollow, that Octavius really planned to be the one and only ruler of the vast Empire, to push Antony into second place and use him to further his own interests.

However much Octavia tried to conciliate husband and brother, she did not succeed. Antony could never shake off the shadow of her difficult brother lurking behind her. If anything, Antony's brief life with Octavia seemed to have lessened his stature in Italy, in contrast to the reputation he had achieved in the East. Such feelings couldn't help but color his attitude toward his wife. If she could be any help at all, she could best be so in Rome, and her home in Rome was the best place for her to have her baby.

Antony now turned his thoughts to Cleopatra, realizing how desperately he needed her and, perhaps, how much he had missed her.

SEVEN

~~~~~~~~~~~~~~~~~~~~~~~~

ANTONY AND CLEOPATRA REUNITED

"Queen of Kings"

Antony hurried to Syria while Octavia sailed back to Rome. As soon as Antony arrived in the Syrian city of Antioch, he sent for Cleopatra. No longer could he delay his Parthian campaign. He needed Cleopatra, not only for her wealth but also for her sound political advice. He looked forward to seeing his twins, and, of course, he looked forward to reuniting with the Queen, whose charm and lively companionship had lost none of their appeal.

Cleopatra didn't hesitate this time but came as quickly as she could, bringing along the three-year-old twins.

Both Antony and Cleopatra had business to discuss: he his much delayed Parthian campaign, she her obsession to put Egypt back on the map and regain her kingdom's lost possessions.

During their stay in Antioch, Cleopatra managed to lure Antony into a bargain of giving back to her most of the lands once owned by her dynasty—Syria, Lebanon (valuable for its cedar trees so needed for building ships), Jordan—all but Judaea, which Antony refused to give her since he had promised it to Herod. In return for his gifts of land, Cleopatra promised to provide Antony with money, food supplies, and a fleet. Having given so many ships to Octavius, Antony needed a new fleet to guard the coastline when he headed for Parthia. It was a good bargain for both.

But this bargain angered Octavius, who thought these provinces should all belong to Rome and be ruled by Roman governors. He blamed Cleopatra's evil influence over her weak, besotted lover. Actually it was part of Antony's wise planning to put loyal local monarchs—not Roman governors, hated in the East for their iron rule and ruthless exploitation of the people—in charge of these lands while he went off to war. Besides, Cleopatra was not considered an evil woman in these regions but rather a most important monarch, looked up to as a goddess-queen.

It was probably at this time that Cleopatra, with

Formal Greek statue of Isis, holding cornucopia.

Antony's approval, gave their twins additional titles. The twin boy was named Alexander Helios ("The Sun"), and the girl Cleopatra Selene ("The Moon"), names that were charged with political significance. Alexander Helios signified the great conqueror as well as the sun god, who, as the source of all light and wisdom, would bring in an era of peace, prosperity, and goodwill. He would usher in a Golden Age and rule jointly with his sister, Cleopatra Selene, the moon goddess. With such grandiose titles, Antony and Cleopatra seemed to be promising that they and their children would be responsible for a new era of peace. Virgil's prediction that Octavia would bear the "son of peace" had not worked out, since she had had only daughters. Antony and Cleopatra were lucky—they already had a son whom they could use in their propaganda to feed the popular longing for peace throughout the Mediterranean world.

This bright outlook for the future was marred by one bone of contention between Antony and Cleopatra—she was annoyed that she had not been given the kingdom of Judaea. She especially wanted access to its valuable plantations of balsam shrubs (used in medicines and perfumes) and the groves of date palms, considered the best in the world. In the past this area had been a source of great profit to her family. Antony would not yield on his promise to Herod but, to placate Cleopatra, agreed to a complicated deal allowing her to collect rent from Herod on these small but valuable areas.

Cleopatra had done well for her country and achieved a special status for it. Unlike other eastern kingdoms,

Egypt was now recognized as a truly equal ally of Rome and was granted Roman protection. It was Cleopatra's wise political as well as administrative ability that inspired a modern Egyptian dramatist to see her as a nationalistic heroine, saving her country from Roman rule and keeping it independent.

In May of 36 B.C. Antony was ready at last to set off, full of hope of defeating the Parthians. The Golden Age of peace would have to wait until they were conquered. Cleopatra accompanied Antony for the first 150 miles, as far as the Euphrates River, the eastern frontier of Syria. There she discovered she was pregnant with a third child by Antony, and turned back toward Alexandria. On her way she stopped in Jerusalem to call on King Herod. It was not like her first, pleasant interview. This time Herod did not conceal his anger with Cleopatra's arrangement to collect rent for the rich balsam and date-palm plantations, giving her, not him, the profit. (Later, false, malicious gossip spread that the Queen had tried to seduce the King and that he had plotted to murder her.)

Back in Alexandria, Cleopatra gave birth to another boy, named Ptolemy Philadelphus, after the most famous king of the dynasty. It was he who had extended the kingdom to its greatest size and glory. She now had three sons: Caesarion, by Caesar; the twin boy; and the new baby. Her apparent ability to produce sons—so important to royalty—was undoubtedly another plus for her in contrast to Octavia.

Cleopatra shared Antony's high hopes of a great victory

in Parthia, which would surely outdo any military glory Octavius could ever hope to win. The Queen even learned the Parthian language in anticipation of ruling that country jointly with Antony.

Antony seemed to plan well and did not make Crassus's mistake of crossing the open plains and deserts beyond the Euphrates River to Parthia. The open country had made it easy for the superb mounted Parthian archers, whose seemingly endless supply of swift horses and arrows had enabled them to harass and defeat the Romans. One of their clever ruses was their famous "Parthian shot"—pretending to flee, they turned in their saddles and shot backward as accurately as forward! They also had armored horsemen who, like medieval knights, could hurl spears while riding at great speed. Romans, who excelled in hand-to-hand fighting or besieging towns, had been thwarted before by the Parthian tactics.

So, though getting a late start because of his repeated trips to accommodate Octavius, Antony thought it wisest to take the more difficult but safer northern route, much of it over winding mountain passes through Armenia. He hoped to reach northern Parthia before winter storms set in. But his high hopes of military victory soon ran into trouble. The slow-moving baggage train—wagons full of vital supplies and siege weapons—could go at only a snail's pace on the narrow mountain trails. While Antony pushed ahead with the main army, the baggage train and its small guard were suddenly attacked and completely destroyed. The King of Armenia, a supposed ally, had turned traitor and alerted the Parthians of its whereabouts.

Without siege engines—battering rams and huge stone-throwing mangonels—Antony was quite helpless and unable to capture any towns. He needed one as a base for food and supplies. Whenever his men foraged for food or went to cut trees to build new siege weapons, the skillful Parthian horsemen would suddenly appear, let loose a volley of arrows, then disappear as quickly as they had come. Bitter cold and winter storms were beginning; starvation threatened. After weeks of getting nowhere, there was nothing to do but retreat.

The retreat through Armenia took twenty-seven days of unspeakable suffering through dense snowstorms. Disease spread, and the enemy continually harassed the weary Roman troops. Thousands of Antony's soldiers either died of dysentery or were killed in surprise attacks. But none of his men blamed their leader, for Antony not only showed great courage in counterattacks but also shared his men's hardships, comforting and trying to help the sick and wounded.

The great dream of victory had failed miserably. When Antony's depleted, exhausted army finally reached Syria, Antony again sent for Cleopatra. The Queen was devastated by the disaster. First she had sought to fulfill her ambitions by her liaison with Caesar, whose life had ended so suddenly and tragically; then she had turned to Antony, who had now failed completely. Her dreams of his being the second Alexander the Great were dashed. Still she remained loyal to him, and she came, bringing what aid and provisions she could to support him and his needy army.

Back in Rome, Octavius seized upon this disaster as good propaganda against the couple. He now began in earnest his smear campaign against Antony and Cleopatra, claiming that Antony's fiasco was due to his hurry to get back to his beloved Queen. And then, in a clever but self-serving gesture, Octavius sent his sister, Octavia, to Athens with 70 ships (a tiny portion of what Antony had given him) and 2,000, instead of the promised 20,000, soldiers. It was planned to look like a generous act on the part of Octavia, but it was her brother's doing. He hoped that his insultingly small gift would lead Antony to finally cast aside his wife and thus further blacken his reputation in Rome.

And as so often with this master politician, his scheme worked out. Poor Octavia again had been used as her brother's tool. Antony did send her back to Rome, where her role as the perfect wife and mother was extolled while Antony was condemned for deserting her for his "oriental" mistress, Cleopatra. Slowly but surely Octavius was underminding Antony's reputation and popularity in Italy, and Antony, far away, could do nothing about it. He could and did, however, lash back with attacks on Octavius's broken promises and unfaithfulness to their partnership. And when Octavius lit into Cleopatra as a harlot and a whore, Antony didn't hesitate to criticize his rival's own sexual conduct, his many extramarital affairs. "Is your wife the only woman you take to bed?" he is said to have asked, accusing his partner of widespread infidelity.

In 34 B.C. Antony was off again to deal with Armenia, whose king had betrayed him on his first expedition. He managed to conquer the kingdom, and the king was brought back to Alexandria as a prisoner. This time Antony returned as victor and put on a celebration in true Alexandrian style, not at all like a Roman military triumph. It was more like a gala show or Dionysian revel, celebrating not only his victory but also Cleopatra's revived ancestral empire.

The celebration went on for days, and climaxed when Cleopatra as Aphrodite-Isis and Antony as Dionysus-Osiris welcomed the citizens in the beautiful Greek gymnasium. They were seated on golden thrones high above the crowd while their children and Cleopatra's son by Caesar sat on silver thrones on a lower level. It was some show, obviously masterminded by Cleopatra. As a modern Alexandrian poet, C. P. Cavafy, wrote,

The Alexandrians are gathered together
to see Cleopatra's children . . .
there to proclaim kings . . .
. . . the day was warm and poetic
the sky a lucid, azure blue . . .
the Alexandrian Stadium
a triumphant achievement of art . . .
and so the Alexandrians rushed to the ceremony . . .
enchanted by the gorgeous spectacle—
knowing full well the worth of all these,
what hollow words these kingships were.

The "kingships" weren't completely worthless, for the

Girls providing musical entertainment at a festival.

masses delighted in glorifying their rulers with divine titles and wide powers. A good show like this gave hopes

of a bright future and gained the people's support, even though it might be only wishful thinking—after all, Parthia was still to be won.

Cleopatra must have had fun dressing up her children

for the occasion in the native costumes of the countries that Antony now bestowed on them. By betrothing them to royal heirs, he hoped to assure their future kingships. Little Alexander Helios, in a white turban adorned with peacock feathers, was declared the future King of Armenia, Media, and Parthia, the vast eastern lands conquered by Alexander the Great. His twin, Cleopatra Selene, the moon goddess, dressed in a flowing Greek dress, would be the future Queen of Cyrene (a small Mediterranean kingdom just west of Egypt) and the island of Crete. Even the two-year-old, though barely able to walk, was costumed in high red boots, a purple robe, and jeweled headdress; he was displayed as the future King of Macedonia, northern Greece and the homeland of Alexander the Great.

Caesarion was proclaimed King of Egypt, to rule jointly with his mother. He was also named King of Kings, while his mother was proclaimed Queen of Kings, affirming that she was the most important monarch in the East. Antony also publicly pronounced that Caesarion was the legitimate son of Julius Caesar—a real jibe at Octavius, and revealing how much Antony still resented his rival's claim to be Caesar's heir.

Not only Octavius but other Romans were naturally incensed at this eastern extravaganza and accused Antony of staging a military Roman triumph (allowed only in Rome) in a foreign city, all to glorify his "oriental" concubine Cleopatra. It did indeed glorify the Queen, but it was quite un-Roman and nonmilitary—the captive King of Armenia was not put to death, as he would have been in a Roman triumph. The show was more a political-religious spectacle than a military procession and was designed to impress the people with their benevolent god-rulers and the glory of Egypt's reinstated power.

Though Antony pronounced all the honors and gifts of land, known as the "Donations of Alexandria," he made no territorial claims for himself. He still considered himself a Roman triumvir, commander of Roman forces in the East. He did, however, relish and cling to his divine title of Dionysus.

The so-called Triumvirate came to an end in 33 B.C. when Octavius, without consulting Antony, finally dismissed the third member. Now the mask was off, and people's fears were heightened that conflict between the two triumvirs, perhaps another bloody civil war, was imminent.

This same year brought political propaganda on both sides to a peak of venom. Octavius was the more clever at this. He and his supporters were gaining success in their campaign to destroy Antony's character, painting him as a traitor to his homeland, a weakling who couldn't control his passion for an evil harlot queen. But knowing Antony's popularity, Octavius was careful not to openly criticize his rival, but to have it appear to come from others. He himself launched his public attacks on Cleopatra. He knew that Romans wouldn't stand another civil war—his war would be against a foreign queen, not against a Roman.

Prophecies and oracles were on the rise too, expressing people's fears and hopes for peace. Like modern political TV ads, they were a powerful influence on the masses.

Most of them originated in the East and were banned in Rome for being subversive. Indeed, they often predicted Rome's downfall before an age of peace could come. Many pointed to Cleopatra as the salvation-bringing Queen, while some pointed to a messiah sent by the sun god. One unique oracle went beyond the fear and hate of Rome to a time of universal peace, when Romans as well as Greeks and all easterners would share the blessings of peace and harmony: "And peace all gentle will come . . . concord and harmony . . . brotherly love between men."

This was the dream of the Golden Age, which Cleopatra and Antony hoped to usher in by uniting East and West under the joint rule of a Roman and a Greek and their children, who were half Roman, half Greek. This dream, based on tolerance of and cooperation with local rulers, would allow the eastern kingdoms to run their internal affairs without interference, as long as they remained loyal.

Such an ideal-sounding arrangement naturally appealed to the East, which feared that Rome planned to be supreme—to be the "policeman of the world," turning all its kingdoms into Roman provinces, making them subjects rather than allies. But whether East and West could ever happily unite was still an unsolved question.

EIGHT

~~~~~~~~~~~~~~~~

THE WARRIOR QUEEN

When the wild Queen was . . .
Plotting destruction to our capital
And ruin to the Empire.
—HORACE, ODES, BOOK I

For the winter of 33–32 B.C., Cleopatra and Antony were settled in Ephesus, an ancient Greek seaport in Asia Minor, recruiting soldiers and support from nearby kingdoms and building ships to be ready if Octavius should declare war. There was no letup in the bitter and vile propaganda that went back and forth between Rome and the East. Political smear campaigns are common in America today, but they pale in viciousness compared to those of the first century B.C.

The anti-Antony propaganda was beginning to take

effect in Italy under Octavius's clever manipulation, but in spite of this Antony still had a surprisingly large number of supporters left in Rome, even in the Senate. At one point a pro-Antony senator made a speech in his favor and denounced Octavius. Infuriated, Octavius appeared at the senate with an armed guard, defended himself, and for the first time openly blasted Antony. This precipitated an extraordinary reaction—200 to 300 of the 900 senators left Rome and sailed off to join Antony in Ephesus. Octavius was glad to see them go—it would make things easier for him to be rid of his rival's followers.

This great show of loyalty to Antony was soon upset by Cleopatra's presence—some of the Roman senators objected to a woman having any part in war preparations. She was always at Antony's side—at councils of war, riding through the streets with him, at dinners with his warrior friends. They advised him that she was hurting his cause and told him he should send her back to Alexandria.

They didn't know Cleopatra. She was enjoying being a warrior queen, supervising the building of a fleet and collecting vital supplies for the army. She flatly refused to leave. And she had some Roman admirers, one of whom spoke on her behalf, saying that it would be unjust not to let a woman who had contributed so much to the war effort share in the glory of the campaign. And, he added, she was in no way inferior in intelligence to any of the other monarchs joining the expedition. Antony, in his devotion to her, his belief in her political astuteness, and his need for her material support and wealth to pay his soldiers, kept her on.

They soon moved their headquarters to the little island of Samos, where their royal allies were assembling for a festival of Dionysus in a kind of previctory celebration. For days music filled the air, dancers twirled in the streets, and theaters were jammed. It made some wonder what sort of victory celebrations Antony and Cleopatra would stage if thcy lavished such festivals on the preparations for war. Though all this hoopla did seem rather premature, Antony and Cleopatra had good reasons to be hopeful. They had the richest part of the Mediterranean world at their command, and Antony was thought to be the best general of his times.

After Samos, Antony and Cleopatra went to Athens, where the Queen was feted and statues of her as Isis were erected in her honor. But the shadow of Octavia hung over Athens, where she and Antony had also been feted not long before. Probably at Cleopatra's urging, Antony now publicly announced his divorcc of Octavia, putting an end to any pretense of friendship with her brother. This was a triumph for Cleopatra, who had long worried that Antony might be persuaded to go back to his Roman wife in order to keep Roman support. Now she felt sure of his devotion and loyalty and his need of her.

Cleopatra and Antony certainly appeared to be husband and wife, but there is no record that they ever married. As a Roman, Antony knew he could not legally marry a foreigner, and he was content to have the Queen, the woman to whom he was more devoted than any other he had ever known, as his mistress. But like Caesar and Cleopatra, who had claimed a sacred union similar to those of gods and goddesses, Antony and Cleopatra probably claimed a sacred marriage that bound them together as the divine rulers, Isis and Dionysus. This gave their children a kind of divine legitimacy, and also pleased the people. No one in the tolerant East seemed to object.

Not so the Romans. Antony's choosing Cleopatra and divorcing Octavia had immediate repercussions and did Antony considerable harm. Several Roman senators now deserted him and went back to Italy, bearing gossipy tales of his enslavement to the foreign Queen—tales of how he massaged her feet at a state banquet, how he interrupted business meetings to read her love notes. Like those who had spread the tale of her swallowing a pearl to show off her wealth, they exaggerated almost beyond belief the lavish feasts, the drinking, and the shows that Cleopatra staged to entertain her lover.

One of the deserters, known for shifting sides to make sure of being with the winner, told Octavius that Antony's will was in Rome. Kept under lock and key, it was well guarded by Rome's high priestesses and not to be opened until after his death. This didn't stop Octavius, who illegally seized it by force and read some selected passages aloud to the senate. No one else ever saw the will, and Octavius may well have tampered with it to suit his own purposes and to further damn his rival. He revealed that Antony and Cleopatra's children were to inherit vast wealth and even, he said, some Roman lands. (Since the children were part foreign and therefore not

Roman citizens, this would have been illegal according to Roman law. Antony would hardly have been so stupid as to put any such statement in a Roman will.) Another passage read aloud by Octavius showed that Antony had asked to be buried in Alexandria with Cleopatra—an unthinkable idea to a Roman and seeming to prove that Antony planned to move the capital from Rome to Alexandria. Octavius knew that this would arouse hostility and imply that Antony was a traitor to Rome.

Slowly but surely Italy was being convinced by Octavius of Antony's treacherous behavior, that Antony had been bewitched by an evil oriental sorceress who worshipped beasts, not gods. Word spread that she was a monster herself, out to destroy not only Antony but, far worse, Rome and its whole empire. So a new element, fear, was added to the propaganda of hate. It went beyond the limits of truth and decency, all created by Octavius as a pretext for war against his former partner so that he could be the sole ruler of the Mediterranean world. But it was Cleopatra who now became Rome's most feared and hated enemy.

Antony had not been back to Italy for five years and didn't fully realize how deeply his reputation had been harmed by his affair with Cleopatra. Nor did he realize that Octavius's top commander, Agrippa, now equaled if not surpassed his own military skills.

At the end of the year 32 B.C., Octavius was ready to call the shots. He dismissed Antony as his co-ruler and deprived him of any Roman office. But he still refrained from declaring war against his former partner—it was not to be publicized as another civil war, Romans fighting

Coin of Cleopatra showing her prominent nose.

Romans. Instead he declared war on the Queen of Egypt. To dramatize the event, he reenacted an ancient Roman ritual. Brandishing a spear dipped in fresh blood from the temple of the war goddess, he hurled it toward the East while his supporters cheered. Cleopatra and Antony had lost the propaganda battle, and only the clash of arms would decide the fate of the Mediterranean world.

NINE

∿∿∿∿∿∿∿∿∿∿∿∿∿∿∿∿∿

THE
BATTLE
OF ACTIUM

❧

What of that Woman, she whose charms
Brought scandal to the Roman arms.
—PROPERTIUS

However confident and hopeful Antony and Cleopatra were, Antony dared not take the offensive and attack Italy with his foreign Queen at his side. The whole country would have risen against him. But, if he abandoned Cleopatra, he would lose Egypt's vital supplies and wealth. Though his soldiers still had faith in Antony's military leadership, more and more they resented Cleopatra's presence—what good could a woman, with her ladies-in-waiting and her many servants, be in the forthcoming battle? Was she going to mastermind the whole campaign?

It was Antony, however, not Cleopatra, who made the decision to make his stand on the west coast of Greece, where he could easily keep in touch with Egypt and protect ships bringing grain to feed his army. Eventually his forces occupied several bases on islands and along the west coast of Greece, facing Italy across the Ionian Sea. The bulk of his fleet and army lay in a well-protected gulf behind a little seaport, Actium.

Antony had a somewhat larger army, but most were not of the caliber of his enemy. Prevented from recruiting soldiers in Italy, he had had to fill out his army with men from the East. Good fighters though they might be, they didn't compare with the well-trained Roman legions, who had the added psychological advantage of believing they were fighting to keep their country from the rule of a feared and hated foreign queen. To begin with, Antony also had a larger fleet, but many of the men manning it lacked experience, whereas Octavius's navy was in top form, well seasoned in naval warfare by recent battles against the Sea King and his pirates.

In the winter of 32–31 B.C., both sides made final preparations, Antony for his defense and Octavius for his offense. Added to propaganda, rumors of omens predicting Antony's downfall were spreading. It was noised about that one of Antony's statues had sweated blood, foretelling his death; another, blown over by violent winds, had smashed to pieces on the ground. Children in the streets of Rome played out the war—Octavius was the winner every time.

While Antony and Cleopatra waited in the gulf for the

enemy to attack, Octavius's commander, Agrippa, managed to slip south and capture their southernmost naval base in Greece. Using this as his own base, he then attacked Antony's other naval supply stations. This was a catastrophic blow to Antony and Cleopatra—Agrippa could now cut off their lifeline of supplies from Egypt. While he was securing these vital areas, Octavius landed his army on the mainland of Greece, setting up camp just north of the opening to the gulf, opposite Antony's camp at Actium.

Soon Antony and Cleopatra realized they were trapped in the gulf—Agrippa's fleet blocked the entrance, only a half mile wide, Octavius's well-protected army menaced from the north, and reinforcements and supplies were completely cut off from the south. Food ran short, and with the hot summer beginning, disease began to spread. The area was unhealthy, swampy, and infested with mosquitoes; soldiers were soon dying of malaria and dysentery. Some began to desert. Antony made several skirmishes, challenging Octavius to battle on land but the latter refused to leave his safe hilltop encampment, well protected by strong walls. He had no desire to confront the skilled soldier Antony in a land battle. He counted on a sea battle and left everything up to his expert naval commander, Agrippa, with his well-equipped fleet.

Food was now dangerously scarce in Antony's camp, and there was little to forage for in this unhealthy region. Many of the rowers died, and their ships, attacked by wood-eating worms, began to rot. Morale sank lower

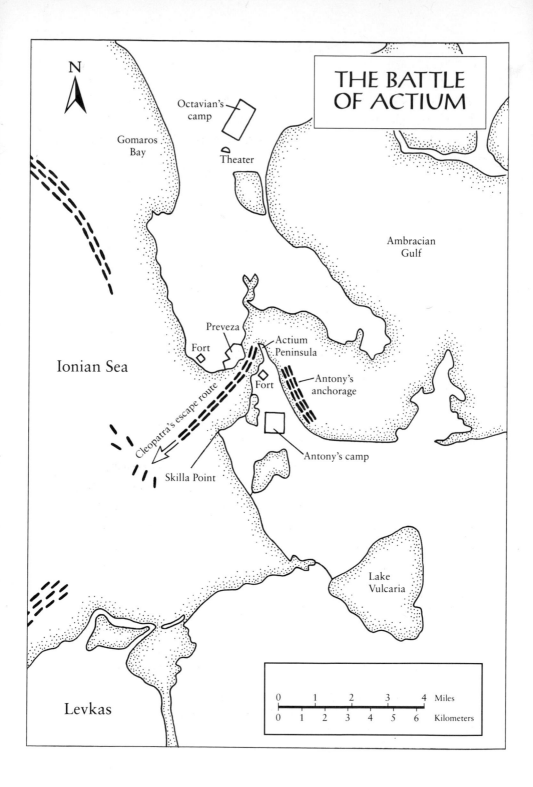

N

THE BATTLE
OF ACTIUM

Octavian's
camp

Theater

Gomaros
Bay

Ambracian
Gulf

Preveza

Fort

Actium
Peninsula

Ionian Sea

Fort

Antony's
anchorage

Cleopatra's escape route

Antony's camp

Skilla Point

Lake
Vulcaria

Levkas

| 0 | 1 | 2 | 3 | 4 | Miles |
| 0 | 1 | 2 | 3 | 4 | 5 | 6 | Kilometers |

and lower and more and more men deserted, revealing to the enemy details of Antony's plight.

By August of 31 B.C., after a failed attempt to break the blockade of enemy ships outside the gulf entrance, things had become so desperate that Antony and Cleopatra called a council of war. Two plans were discussed— one to abandon the fleet and retreat inland over the mountains to eastern Greece, the other to fight their way out by ship and hope to escape to Egypt. Antony's right-hand commander argued for the land retreat, reminding Antony that he was better skilled at land warfare than at sea. Cleopatra argued that to take a weakened army over the high mountain passes would make no sense—even if some made it, Octavius would command the seas and prevent their getting back to their supply base, Egypt. But if they could get what ships they had back to Egypt, they could make a new stand against the enemy with a reinforced army. Cleopatra couldn't bear to abandon her fleet, which would mean losing not only all her ships but also her much-needed treasure, carefully hidden in her flagship. Realizing the odds against them and considering their desperate situation, Antony knew her arguments made sense. It was decided that he and Cleopatra, with as many ships as possible,

Both sides wanted the open sea—the enemy to use its much larger fleet to outflank Antony's, Antony to carry out his plan to escape by sail when the breeze was at its peak.

Soon ships at each end of the crescent were battling while the weak center continued to thin out, giving Cleopatra her chance to sail through and escape to Egypt.

would try to escape by sea while the rest of the army would retreat inland over the mountainous route. This decision precipitated another desertion—a supposedly loyal friend went off to the enemy and revealed Antony's dilemma and the depleted strength of his forces.

Due to the ravages of death and disease, Antony found he was short of trained rowers to man his ships, so he set fire to the ones he could not use, reducing his fleet to 170 ships, Cleopatra's to 60: 230 ships in all. Octavius had more than 400. Since Antony no longer aimed at an impossible victory but at escape, he loaded his ships with sails, unusual in a naval battle and a heavy, bulky burden to the rowers. Antony surely would not have inflicted this cumbersome burden unless he was preparing for flight. Some think that the burden of the sails so disheartened his crews that many surrendered right away. Cleopatra was put in command of what remained of her fleet.

Stormy weather delayed their scheme a few days, and the weather was all-important in the escape plan. On a good summer day Antony knew he could count on an afternoon northwesterly breeze for sailing swiftly southeast—the square-rigged ships of the day could sail only before the wind.

September 2 dawned bright and clear, the sea blue, and calm as glass. Antony's fleet set out of the harbor and strung out in a crescent formation, with the best-manned ships at either end, the weakest in the center. Cleopatra's ships were behind this center, lined up near the mouth of the gulf. The enemy, no longer blocking the gulf entrance, faced them in a similar line-up about a mile away. Their plan now was to lure Antony's ships out to the open sea, where, spread out, they could be more easily attacked by the enemy's much larger fleet.

The ships of both sides were similar, with metal ramming prows and their sides reinforced with iron-bound timbers to resist ramming. While soldiers manned the decks, slingers and archers stood in towers at bow and stern. The larger ships had three rows of oars and several rowers to an oar.

Each side rested its oars, hoping the other would move first. Then the expected breeze, very gently at first, began to blow, and Antony's fleet moved. Agrippa's plan to draw Antony's ships far out from land was working, and soon the two end wings of the fleets' crescents were battling, ramming each other while arrows and rocks from catapults flew from one boat to another. Antony's fleet was outnumbered nearly two to one, and the enemy had more small, maneuverable ships that could dart, ram, and dash away unharmed. Sometimes huge iron grappling hooks were used to pull an enemy ship close enough to board it and engage in hand-to-hand combat, preferred by the Romans.

Though Antony was waiting for a special moment to carry out his plan of escape, he and his squadron had been drawn into a hard fight as Agrippa's speedy ships closed in, attacking from all sides. Soon they were grappling at close quarters with Agrippa's fleet. Decks became slippery with blood and saltwater.

The battle had been going on for less than two hours

when the wind picked up speed. This was the moment Cleopatra and Antony had counted on. Leading her fleet in her flagship, Cleopatra sailed into the open sea, and while fighting on the wings intensified, she slipped through an opening in the thinned-out center—just as she and Antony had planned. Antony immediately left his huge, unwieldy flagship and switched to a small, fast vessel. Raising his sails, he sped after Cleopatra with the brisk wind behind him. Forty of his fleet were able to break free and join their leader. Unfortunately, the others could not get loose and were soon overcome by the many more and better-manned enemy ships. Some of Antony's were sunk; the rest surrendered.

The enemy, surprised at this sudden turn of events, later blamed it on the treachery of the depraved and cowardly Queen, whose besotted lover abandoned his fleet and his honor in his lust to follow her. In reality the two had carried out their plan and saved about 100 out of 230 ships, as well as Cleopatra's much-needed treasure. They still had hopes of fighting another day with renewed forces. They had lost a battle but not necessarily the war.

Antony didn't yet know that the other part of his plan—for the commander of his land forces to escape over the mountain passes and go on to Egypt—had failed utterly. Stopped by Octavius's legions, who offered good terms in exchange for their surrender, most of these half-starved soldiers couldn't resist and joined the enemy. Only Antony's loyal commander and a small contingent managed to escape by night. The loss of his land forces was a far worse blow for Antony and Cleopatra than their loss of a few ships.

But later Roman poets, praising Octavius, made the battle of Actium, which was really only a fight to escape, into the greatest naval battle of all times.

Catching up to Cleopatra's squadron, Antony boarded her flagship, and they sailed on to the tip of southern Greece. There he got word of his land forces' surrender. This final blow was almost more than he could bear. He began to brood and think of suicide. He sat apart, not speaking to anyone, a broken man who had lost his standing as a great leader and Roman commander.

TEN

~~~~~~~~~~~~~~~~~~~~~~~~

CLEOPATRA'S DEATH

Give me my robe, put on my crown,
I have immortal longings in me.
—SHAKESPEARE'S *ANTONY AND CLEOPATRA*,
ACT V, SCENE II

Actium had hardly been the great naval victory it was later blown up to be, but it had been decisive as to who would rule the Mediterranean world. In his heart Antony knew this. He continued in his melancholy aloofness for some time.

Not Cleopatra. With a bit of bravado, she sailed into the harbor of Alexandria with flags flying and music playing as though returning from a victory. She may have felt some sense of victory in having escaped with a considerable portion of her fleet intact, but she also felt that a show of triumph would dispel any attempt by political enemies who might otherwise use the disaster at Actium as an excuse to revolt. She had any suspected of treachery put to death. Luckily she could count on the loyalty of her Egyptian subjects, those living mostly beyond the city on the upper Nile, who offered to take up arms in her defense.

With characteristic energy the Queen set to work to build more ships, recruit forces, and plan new schemes to keep her own and her kingdom's independence. She knew it was only a matter of time before Octavius would appear, eager to grab Egypt and above all her treasure.

Aside from preparing for defense, she contemplated a wild backup scheme of flight—to sail to far-off India, where she had trade connections. First she sent her son Caesarion, whom she wanted to keep from harm at all costs, up the Nile River and across the desert to the southern end of the Red Sea. Then she arranged to convey some of her fleet overland to the northern end of the sea. Though the distance was only twenty miles, it was a difficult undertaking—putting the boats on frames, then having them hauled on rollers by hundreds of workers. If later she had to resort to this plan, she would join her fleet and sail south on the Red Sea, pick up her son, and go on with him to India, where they would set up a new kingdom! She actually succeeded in getting her ships overland to the Red Sea, but then her enterprise was foiled. The native Arabs there had all gone over to Octavius—they burned and destroyed the entire fleet.

Every day the news grew more disheartening, with tales of more and more desertions to the enemy—the increasing desertions of his soldiers must have been the cruellest blow in Antony's life. King Herod of Jerusalem, who owed his crown and kingdom to Antony, not only deserted but provided Octavius with supplies and reinforcements for his attack on Alexandria. One of the few men who remained loyal to Antony and Cleopatra was the commander they had left near Actium, but most of his army gradually went over to the enemy, thinking it offered a safer, more advantageous future.

Antony, still devoted to his soldiers, generously released any who wanted to leave him, paid them handsomely, and sent them on their way. He and Cleopatra now realized that their only options were to defend their city as best they could or to negotiate with Octavius.

Among the several proposals Cleopatra sent to Octavius was her offer to give up her crown if he would allow her children to inherit it. Octavius's answer was somewhat evasive but suggested she could expect kind treatment if she put Antony to death. Antony proposed to surrender and retire as a private citizen if Octavius would spare Cleopatra. He got no response, and all attempts at negotiation failed.

In a kind of grim foreboding of death, Antony and Cleopatra revived their old group of high livers, renamed it "Partners in Death," and had a last fling of wild parties in defiance of their inner despair. To show despair would be a sign of weakness and defeat, and Cleopatra was not ready to admit defeat. Besides, feasting and dancing would be helpful in raising the spirits of their friends and followers.

By the end of July of the year 30 B.C., Octavius was in

the suburbs of Alexandria. Antony challenged his enemy with a few ships in the harbor and his cavalry on the land. His fleet soon went over to the enemy, but he had a minor victory with his horsemen. This emboldened him to challenge Octavius to settle things by single combat. Personal fighting courage was not one of Octavius's strong points. He scornfully refused.

The only thing left for Antony was one last attempt to fight the enemy with whatever forces and ships he could muster. The night before this desperate effort Antony dined with friends and soldiers. He told his friends that he no longer counted on victory but rather on an honorable death. So he ate and drank heavily, knowing it might be his last dinner. Some of the soldiers wept to hear him talk that way. Yet fear and foreboding of what the morrow might bring to their leader and the beautiful city of Alexandria were spreading rapidly.

An old legend that gods forsake a city before its fall revived. It was said that at midnight, when the city was quiet, its people dejected by fear of the morrow, the silence was suddenly broken by exquisite sounds of all kinds of musical instruments and voices singing. It sounded like a troop of Dionysian revelers singing as they danced wildly right through the middle of the city to the outer gate that led to the enemy camp. Here the noise grew to a frenzied crescendo, then abruptly ceased and passed away.

The legend's coming true was seen as a sign that Antony's favorite god, Dionysus, had abandoned him and his city, causing the downfall of the popular god-king Antony-Dionysus.

In his poem, "The God Abandons Antony," the Alexandrian poet C. P. Cavafy addresses Antony, poignantly retelling the old legend:

> *When suddenly at the midnight hour*
> *an invisible troupe is heard passing*
> *with exquisite music, with shouts—*
> *do not mourn in vain your fortune failing you*
>   *now,*
> *your works that have failed, the plans of your life*
> *that have all turned to be illusions.*
> *. . . listen with emotion, . . .*
> *a last enjoyment . . . to the sounds*
> *the exquisite instruments of the mystical troupe,*
> *and bid farewell, the Alexandria you are losing.*

The next day, August 1, seemed to verify the gloomy foreboding. Antony's fleet sailed out of the harbor to confront the enemy's. Instead of attacking, they joined the enemy fleet and sailed back to attack the city, while Antony and his few soldiers watched in horror. Then his cavalry panicked and also joined the enemy. Antony and his small force resisted for a short time but were soon pushed back into the city. It was said that as he rushed into the palace he cried, "Cleopatra has betrayed me." Perhaps in the blackness of despair and final defeat, he did utter some such words. More likely it was enemy propaganda, and in any case it was not true—the deserters went over to the enemy from their own self-interest, for a safer, more secure life with the winner, who they knew would reward them handsomely.

Cleopatra was not in the palace when Antony rushed in—she had retreated to her mausoleum, just barely finished; the tomb stood on hallowed ground next to the sacred temple of Isis. With Cleopatra were her hairdresser, Iras; her lady-in-waiting, Charmian; and her fabled treasure. The heavy doors were securely bolted. She must guard her treasure from Octavius, whom she knew was bent on laying hands on it. Her treasure might be her last bargaining ploy to buy her children's rights to the throne of Egypt, or at least their right to live. If that failed, she was ready to burn the entire treasure with the wood and other highly flammable materials already heaped around it.

Then a rumor that Cleopatra had committed suicide spread through the city, perhaps suggested by her retreat into her monumental tomb. When Antony heard the rumor, he felt he had nothing more to live for. Distressed that he had lagged behind Cleopatra in courage, he asked his servant to kill him. The obedient servant drew his sword as though to carry out the deed, but suddenly turned away and stabbed himself instead. At this, Antony grabbed another sword and plunged it into his belly. But the wound did not kill him immediately. Though bleeding profusely, he was still conscious when a messenger arrived to say Cleopatra was still alive.

The dying Antony asked that he be taken to her, so as to die in her arms. Two slaves carried him to Cleopatra's mausoleum, but getting him into it proved difficult. The well-barricaded doors could not be opened quickly enough. But from an unfinished upper window Cleopatra and her two women let down ropes, which Antony's slaves somehow tied around him. Then with great effort, Cleopatra, aided by her two women, managed to pull him up and get him safely inside. The Queen laid him on a couch, wailing and tearing her hair, even lacerating her breasts in anguish. Covered with blood and grappling with death, Antony stretched his arms out lovingly toward her. She gave him a glass of wine which enabled him to gasp out his last words to her, begging her not to grieve over his bad fortune but to remember past happiness and glories, and that he had fallen "not ignobly, a Roman, conquered by a Roman." He died in her arms.

Someone hurried off to Octavius with the news, taking Antony's blood-stained sword as proof. Octavius reacted quickly and sent a trusted friend, Proculius, to arrest Cleopatra and, above all, prevent her from destroying her treasure. Unable to open the door, Proculius talked to the queen through a small grating and, while conversing, noticed the open upper window where Antony had been pulled in. Reporting this to Octavius, he was soon back with another man, who this time engaged the Queen in conversation so that Proculius, unnoticed, could climb up a ladder to the open window. The Queen was talking at the grate when Proculius suddenly bounded in and seized her from behind. She quickly reached for a dagger hidden in her dress, but her captor snatched it before she could use it. He pronounced her under arrest, a prisoner of the Romans. This was the final humiliation, a fate worse than death. She shuddered at the thought of a Roman triumph where she might be paraded, bound in chains, through the streets of Rome before a vulgar jeering crowd.

With the treasure safe, Octavius had his prisoner moved to the palace, where, shattered in spirit and worried about the fate of her children, she fell ill with a fever. Her breasts became inflamed and infected from the wounds she had inflicted on herself when Antony was dying.

Then Octavius came to call on her—the first face-to-face meeting of the two enemies. He knew he could never relax as long as Cleopatra lived. But if he paraded her in his Roman triumph and executed her afterward, as was the Roman custom for important prisoners, he might damage his reputation and be accused of excessive cruelty to a woman. He remembered the crowd's sympathy for Cleopatra's young sister, Arsinoë, when she was shown in Caesar's triumph. Better, he thought, if the Queen would do away with herself. So, knowing that Cleopatra would rather die than be paraded at his Roman triumph, he did nothing to dispel her fear that that was indeed his plan. He also informed her that he was about to annex Egypt, ruining her entire life's work for its independence. Her power and glory had come to an end. Ill and distraught, she fell on her knees, begging mercy for her children. Her victor was coldly evasive, and Cleopatra realized there was only one way out.

Octavius soon reduced her guards and sent them word to turn a blind eye to any attempt at suicide. He allowed her two women attendants to stay with her. But getting impatient for news of a suicide, he sent a messenger to warn her that he planned to leave for Rome in three days, taking her and her children with him. Cleopatra requested and was granted permission to pay a last visit to Antony's tomb, where she laid some flowers and told her

Cleopatra's death scene, showing her contemplating the deadly cobra. In reality she was fully dressed.

dead lover that she hoped to be buried with him, that they would be united in death as they had been in life. Back in her mausoleum she prepared for the kind of death she felt suitable for the Queen of Egypt. It would be her last spectacle.

She sent a letter to her conqueror, requesting to be buried at Antony's side. Octavius knew then that she had decided to put an end to her life. Publicly feigning concern, he sent men to investigate. True to her character, Cleopatra had arranged a dramatic and unforgettable death scene which she carried out calmly and courageously despite her illness and concern over the fate of her children. At least Caesarion, she hoped, had safely escaped. After bathing, she dressed herself exquisitely as the Queen of Egypt–goddess Isis and lay down on a sumptuous golden couch to partake of her last meal. By the time Octavius's men reached her, she was already dead. Her hairdresser, Iras, lay dead at her feet; her lady-in-waiting, Charmian, almost dead, was trying to adjust the Queen's crown topped by the image of the sacred Egyptian cobra, symbol of everlasting life.

"Was this right, Charmian?" cried out one of the men. "It is entirely right," came the faint answer, "and fitting for a queen descended from so many kings." Then Charmian, too, fell dead.

But just how Cleopatra died has never been fully resolved. There were no dagger marks, so it must have been poison—perhaps, as some thought, concealed in her comb. It is more likely and fitting that she used a venomous snake, which according to one story was smuggled to her in a basket of figs by a loyal friend (could it have been the same friend who had smuggled her into Caesar's presence?). It was said that two faint traces of punctures were visible on her arm. Though no snake was found in her tomb, people claimed they saw tracks of one on the nearby beach. If she died by snakebite, she would have used the sacred hooded cobra, symbol of royalty and long associated with Isis and immortality. The story as told by Plutarch refers to an asp, but we now know that the cobra of the Nile River was called the Egyptian asp. The ordinary venemous asp is a

The cobra or Egyptian asp, thought to be the cause of Cleopatra's death.

small viper whose bite causes nausea, disfiguring ugly swellings on the skin, and a painful, lingering death. But the bite of a cobra merely causes drowsiness, then a coma and a painless death. Surely Cleopatra would have chosen the cobra for its royal and religious connections, as well as for its assurance of a dignified end to her life.

Cleopatra's death—she was thirty-nine years old—impressed even her enemies, who seemed to think it her one and only redeeming act, a glorious end to a depraved life. The Roman poet Horace, after describing her evil ways and her cowardly flight from the battle of Actium, changed his tone completely when he wrote of her death:

> Yet she preferred a finer style of dying:
> She did not, like a woman, shirk the dagger
>   Or seek by speed at sea
> To change her Egypt for obscurer shores,
>
> But gazing on her desolated palace
> With a calm smile, unflinchingly laid hand on
>   The angry asps until
> Her veins had drunk the deadly poison deep:
>
> And, death determined, fiercer then than ever,
> Perished. Was she to grace a haughty triumph,
>   Dethroned . . . ? Not Cleopatra.
>
> —ODES, BOOK I

ELEVEN

~~~~~~~~~~~~~~~~~~~~~~~~~~~~

AFTERMATH

*Alone of Alexander the Great's successors,
she became a legend, like Alexander himself.*
—W. W. TARN

C leopatra was spared the news that her adored son Caesarion had been murdered even before her suicide. His whereabouts betrayed, he was overtaken escaping to the Red Sea and brought back to Alexandria, where Octavius, warned that "too many Caesars were not a good thing," had him put to death immediately. He was only sixteen. Cleopatra and Antony's three little children, too young to be a threat, were spared but later had to march in the triumphal parade in Rome behind the effigy of their mother laid out on a golden couch, replete with snakes entwining her arm.

After formally annexing Egypt, which he would guard jealously as his own private property, Octavius granted clemency to those who did not threaten him—many were former followers of Antony. He granted Cleopatra's request that she be buried next to Antony and was even persuaded (with a huge bribe) by one of her admirers to leave her statues standing. However, he tore down all of Antony's—there was to be no trace left of this rival. He was invited to visit Alexandria's beautiful temples but refused, saying that he worshipped gods, not bulls!

While still in Alexandria, Octavius treated the memory of his enemy the Queen with outward respect—he dared not do otherwise, for she was deeply mourned by many; they felt that they had lost a champion who had spent much of her life fighting to keep her country independent of Rome's iron rule. As late as the seventh century A.D., an Egyptian bishop said that he could think of no other woman or monarch who had ever surpassed her.

But in Rome and in the West, Cleopatra's reputation was quite the opposite; the propaganda smears against her as an infamous woman whose greatest interest was sexual lust and debauchery remained. This one-sided Roman image of such a remarkably intelligent and capable woman is unfortunately the one we have inherited, since our western culture and historical knowledge have come to us mostly from Rome. That there was quite a different appraisal of Cleopatra in the East is rarely glimpsed— there she was known as *the* Queen, and shrines were set up in her honor. Like Alexander the Great, she became a legend, and was honored in the East if damned in the West.

Though Cleopatra's image both in art and in drama has gone through some transformations in the last two thousand years, her role as the evil seductress has rarely changed; she both threatens and allures, and men seem to like her that way. Her death scene has been a favorite of artists, who could not resist painting her lying naked or half naked on a couch with snakes entwining her, whereas in reality she was fully dressed in her royal robes and there probably was only one large snake.

Women see in her a symbol of sensual delight—you can buy "Cleopatra" soap, face cream, or perfume and hope to capture some of her alluring glamor. Many a nightclub that features belly dancing displays the name "Cleopatra." A tourist guide in southern Turkey will gladly show you Cleopatra's beach of fine white sand, where she and Antony supposedly spent many a moonlit night! But it seems more important to remember her as a courageous and ambitious woman fighting for her country's independence and the preservation of Greek and Egyptian culture. She was a woman of strong intelligence and political keenness, a queenly character with a sense of beauty and love of art, a scholar of literature and philosophy.

The verdict of history—that Octavius (soon to be called Caesar Augustus) deserved to win, that Rome was destined to rule the Mediterranean world—was right in the sense that Octavius, though less noble and appealing than Antony, turned out to be an extraordinarily able ruler and statesman once he had gotten rid of his enemies. Retaining most of Antony's wise arrangements in the Middle East, he created a machinery of government forever famous for its law and order. Since the winner takes all, Octavius reaped the benefit of the longed-for peace that came at last. Peace and prosperity mattered more to the people than the outworn republican slogans of freedom, long since dead in any case. Rome might never have agreed to Antony and Cleopatra's ideal of an equal partnership between East and West. Would Cleopatra have shared Antony's power in Rome, or would Alexandria have been the new seat of government? Rome would not have accepted either without another war. Rome had to be supreme.

Even if the image of Cleopatra as a lustful, depraved siren outdid all other images of the Queen, some intangible hint of her greatness always lurked beneath her tarnished reputation. Her courage could not be denied, and the fact that Rome so feared her was proof of her political power. And though her enemies construed her lovely voice, her charm, and her vivacity as the wiles of a sorceress, was there not, perhaps, some lingering doubt that maybe she was instead an exceptional woman, a woman ahead of her time?

AUTHOR'S NOTE

With so few records left, with such false and vituperative Roman propaganda against her, with so much legend surrounding her, Cleopatra remains something of an enigma. It is too bad that there are so few comments from her scholarly or artistic friends in Alexandria. Perhaps someday more papyrus scrolls will turn up to fill the gaps of missing episodes—such as just how and by what route she escaped to Syria when her brother's guardians tried to depose her, or how she survived the soldiers' camp life at Actium in the unhealthy mosquito-ridden area during a long, hot summer. Such missing details would help flesh out her life and help us to know her better.

I have mostly relied on well researched biographies of Cleopatra for the perspective I used to portray her character, her hopes, and her ambitions. These modern biographers have looked beyond Roman sources and found quite different points of view on the Queen in Arab and Egyptian sources.

We know her reputation, some good, mostly bad. But as Shakespeare wrote, "age cannot wither her," and neither can all the two thousand years since her death.

—P. S. B.

CHRONOLOGY

332 b.c. Alexander the Great captures Egypt. Begins to build city of Alexandria.

323 B.C. Alexander dies, and his general and relative, Ptolemy, takes over Egypt and begins rule of Ptolemy Dynasty, which lasts until 30 B.C.

80 B.C. Ptolemy XII, known as the "Flute Player," King of Egypt, father of Cleopatra, assumes rule.

69 B.C. Cleopatra born.

59 B.C. Ptolemy XII goes to Rome for military help against uprisings in Alexandria.

58 B.C. Ptolemy returns to Egypt, is restored to power.

55 B.C. Ejected from Alexandria, Ptolemy again goes to Rome for aid.

53 B.C. Romans defeated by Parthians.

51 B.C. Ptolemy XII dies. Cleopatra becomes Queen and her brother Ptolemy XIII King as joint rulers of Egypt.

Cleopatra assumes sole rule.

49 B.C. Cleopatra exiled by brother and his guardians,

takes refuge in Syria.

Julius Caesar returns to Rome after great military conquest of Gaul.

48 B.C.   Civil War between Roman leaders Caesar and Pompey. Caesar pursues Pompey to Egypt, only to find him murdered. Caesar stays on, helps Cleopatra regain throne by fighting her brother, who is drowned trying to escape. Cleopatra and youngest brother, Ptolemy XIV, made King and Queen.

47 B.C.   Caesar returns to Rome. Cleopatra gives birth to their son, Caesarion.

46 B.C.   Caesar celebrates military triumphs in Rome. Cleopatra, Ptolemy, and Caesarion come to Rome.

44 B.C.   Murder of Caesar. Cleopatra returns to Egypt. Young Ptolemy dies or is murdered.

42 B.C.   Mark Antony, Octavius, and Lepidus form second Triumvirate and defeat Caesar's assassins.

41 B.C.   Cleopatra joins Antony in Tarsus, goes back with him to winter in Egypt.

40 B.C.   Parthians attack Syria. Tension between Antony and Octavius eased by Antony's marriage to sister Octavia. Cleopatra gives birth to twins by Antony.

39 B.C.   To prepare war on Parthians, Antony moves Octavia to Athens.

37 B.C.   Antony and Octavius make new treaty to prolong Triumvirate. Antony sends Octavia back to Rome, rejoins Cleopatra.

36 B.C.   Antony fails in attack on Parthians. Cleopatra's

third child by Antony born. Octavius dismisses Lepidus from Triumvirate.

34 B.C. Antony invades Armenia and captures the King. "Donations of Alexandria" celebrated, with gifts of land and titles to Cleopatra and her children.

33 B.C. Propaganda war between Octavius and Antony and Cleopatra begins.

32 B.C. Antony divorces Octavia. Octavius seizes Antony's will and publishes its alleged contents. War between Antony and Octavius imminent, but to avoid war between Romans, Octavius declares war on Cleopatra.

31 B.C. Antony and Cleopatra set up military bases on west coast of Greece.

Octavius's admiral Agrippa storms these bases, cuts off all food supplies from Egypt.

Battle of Actium. Antony and Cleopatra escape to Egypt.

30 B.C. Octavius conquers Egypt. Suicides of Antony and Cleopatra.

NOTES

INTRODUCTION:
Cleopatra's World

Plutarch is the most colorful ancient writer of Cleopatra's life and character. He had the advantage of hearing firsthand descriptions of the Queen from his grandfather, who lived in Alexandria during her lifetime. So his knowledge of her looks and personality are thought to be genuine. Some details of her death were told to his grandfather by Cleopatra's personal physician. But Plutarch, born about 100 years after her death when the Roman Empire controlled all the eastern Mediterranean world, based most of his writing on Roman prejudice against Antony and Cleopatra. More interested in morals than history, Plutarch was often historically inaccurate and often contradictory. (See Plutarch's *The Lives of the Noble Grecian and Romans*, p. 757 in Great Books Edition.)

Alexander the Great. See M. Grant's *From Alexander to Cleopatra* for the importance of Alexander's far-flung conquests—modern Turkey, Armenia, Syria, Iran, Iraq, and Egypt—which changed the whole Middle East into one empire of Greek culture. Though he introduced kingship to the democratic Greeks and was responsible for the religious cult of diefying rulers, he encouraged the spread of Greek thought. The period between Alexander and Cleopatra has been neglected, eclipsed by the earlier Greek classical period. But this period should be recognized for its own achievements, its great advances in science, medicine and mathematics.

Alexandria. Of Alexandria's great buildings the most famous were the Pharos Lighthouse, the library, and the museum, where extraordinary scientific discoveries were made by the Greeks—the astronomer Aristarchus discovered that the sun, not the earth was the center of the universe, Eratosthenes figured out the circumference of the world, and the mathematician Euclid created the system of geometry that we still use. Here, too, the architect-engineer Sostraties designed the great Pharos Lighthouse and Sosigenes the solar calendar. Dissection of corpses led to medical advances. (See E. M. Forster's *Alexandria: A History and Guide*, pp. 19, 40–47, which is concise and entertaining. Also see E. Bradford's *Cleopatra*, pp. 47–49, for details of the lighthouse, and M. Grant's *Cleopatra*, pp. 9, 32–33.)

CHAPTER 1:

Cleopatra Grows Up

The Sibylline Oracles in Cleopatra's time were a collection of underground political prophecies from the Near East. Though Rome had its own Sibylline Books often doctored for political purposes, it banned the eastern ones as subversive. The ones quoted throughout the book were largely eastern and anti-Roman, predicting that Roman rule would end with the arrival of a savior in the East. Many seemed to point to Cleopatra as the savior. They became a popular form of propoganda, spreading hope of freedom from Rome's iron rule. The term Sibylline stems from Sibyl, an ancient prophetess whose origin is unknown. Like the famous Greek prophetess at Delphi, she uttered enigmatic sayings that were interpreted as valuable prophecies and highly esteemed. (See J. Lindsay's *Cleopatra* pp. 355–380 and M. Grant's *Cleopatra*.

Dionysus (Bacchus to the Romans) was much more to the Greeks than just the god of wine. Originally a fertility god, he had also brought the arts of civilization to mankind, and he offered a mystical, religious goal for the truly pious to escape worldly bonds for a more spiritual life and salvation after death. Dionysus became a sort of patron saint of Alexandria. (See M. Grant's *Cleopatra,* pp. 22–24.)

The Roman Republic was really more of an oligarchy than a democracy, ruled mostly by a group of aristocrats who made up the senate. For a long time the much revered senators ruled wisely and justly, but when the people began to agitate for more equal voting rights, they objected. Through uprisings the people finally won a measure of democratic equality—but more in theory than in practice. Senators managed to remain the real rulers of the state. But by Cleopatra's time, the long-revered senators had been corrupted by Rome's expansion overseas and the wealth they were able to extort from new provinces. Greed for money and power began to undermine old Republican ideals. Roman farmers, forced to leave their farms and go to war, were replaced by prisoners-of-war who provided slave labor. Military heroes were on the rise and gained more and more power. Rome was becoming an empire under one-man military rule. (See E. Goltz Huzar's *Mark Antony*, pp. 3–11, for a clear, concise summary of the history of the Republic, and Brooks and Walworth's *When the World Was Rome*, p. 18 and chapters 5 and 6.)

Brother-sister marriages were not a Greek but an age-old Egyptian custom and were introduced to Alexandria by the second King Ptolemy. (The first King Ptolemy had married a Syrian princess outside the royal family, perhaps accounting for Cleopatra's slightly Syrian looks.) Ptolemy II adopted the Egyptian custom to fit royalty's divine titles and keep its purity. Greeks came to tolerate brother-sister marriages in a religious sense. They had models among their own gods and goddesses, such as their great god Zeus, who had married his sister Hera just as the Egyptian god Osiris had married his sister Isis. So this type of marriage was accepted as sacred or divine, if not strictly legal. (See M. Grant's *Cleopatra*, pp. 26–29.)

Isis. The fullest account of Isis and her widespread influence is a recent book *Isis in the Greco-Roman World* by R. E. Witt, who aims to show how much the goddess influenced Christianity and how closely she resembled the Virgin Mary with her attributes of love, mercy, and forgiveness. Like Mary, she was a virgin who had given birth to a divine son and was often depicted holding her baby just like Mary held baby Jesus. Christianity, so soon burst upon the world, drew much from the cult of Isis but found her also a serious rival.

Notes

〜〜〜〜〜〜〜〜〜〜〜

CHAPTER 2:
Cleopatra's Visit to the Nile

Hymn to the Nile. The excerpt from an ancient Egyptian hymn to the Nile shows the people's reverence for the Nile River, whose annual flooding seemed a life-giving miracle and was honored with festivals and sacrifices. (See L. Casson's *Ancient Egypt*, p. 30, for the Nile geography, and p. 36 for the Hymn to the Nile.)

Egyptian religion. See L. Casson's *Ancient Egypt*, pp. 71–80, a good explanation of Egyptian religion from earliest times showing Egyptian love and concern for animals and nature, Egyptian tolerance, and even its momentary rise to a belief in only one god, under the Pharaoh Akhenaten.

CHAPTER 5:
Antony and Cleopatra

Artemesia, a widowed queen of the ancient city Halicarnassus (modern Bodrum of Turkey), had been alerted of an enemy naval attack and hid her own fleet in a secret harbor. When the enemy sailed into the main harbor and went ashore to carouse, she secretly sailed forth with her ships and captured the enemy fleet; putting her own sailors aboard, she sailed off in the enemy ships to their island home of Rhodes. Taking the island by surprise—and to its humiliation—she had completely reversed the anticipated capture of a queen and her kingdom. She must have been an inspiration to Cleopatra. (See G. E. Bean's *Turkey Beyond Meander: An Archeological Guide*, pp. 106–107.)

Mark Antony. For more on his relationship to Cleopatra, see

E. Goltz Huzar's *Mark Antony*, pp. 190–191, which suggests
that there was a passionate love affair for a while, but that
they stayed together because they ultimately needed each
other. And see pp. 253–257 on Antony's character, his short-
comings as well as his nobility, his faithfulness and kindness
to friends and his aims for a united East and West. (See
R. Syme's *Roman Revoution*, p. 274, for a different view,
doubting they were ever in love, and asserting that it was only
his loyalty to the Queen that kept him tied to her.)

Cleopatra's barge is first described by Plutarch, and the description enhanced by Shakespeare in his play *Antony and
Cleopatra* with even more dramatic overtones. (Act II, scene
2. See also Plutarch's *Lives*.)

CHAPTER 6:
Antony Abandons Cleopatra

Herod the Great, King of Judaea, is perhaps most famous for
the Slaughter of the Innocents at the time of Jesus Christ. A
handsome, ambitious man, he allied himself with the Romans
and was made King of Judaea by Antony in exchange for help
against the Parthians. He was as ruthless and scheming as
were most rulers of that turbulent first century B.C. He put to
death most of his ten wives and several of his sons. For his bitter quarrel with Cleopatra over lands both coveted, see M.
Grant's *Cleopatra*, pp. 127–129, 139–141, 160; and, on his
deserting Antony for Octavius, see p. 219.

CHAPTER 7:
Antony and Cleopatra Reunited

Cleoptra's trip with the army. There is no record of how

Cleopatra traveled with Antony and his army the 150 miles from Antioch to the Euphrates River—by horseback, chariot, or litter. A litter would have been too slow. I suspect she rode in a chariot with Antony or on horseback at his side. Some have claimed that she planned to go the whole way to Parthia and turned back only upon finding she was pregnant.

Antony's celebration of his victories, known as **The Donations of Alexandria**, have caused much controversy. His enemies claimed he was giving away Roman provinces to Cleopatra and her children, others deny this and claim that he gave only eastern territories, keeping on their local rulers. But did his betrothals of the children to eastern rulers mean he planned to have them future rulers or were they just to cement loyalty and friendship? Not many people were bothered by this arrangement, except Octavius, who used it against Antony. What most upset Octavius on this occasion was Antony's public announcement that Caesarion was Caesar's legitimate son and heir, refuting Octavius's claim to that role. (See J. M. Carter *The Battle of Actium*, pp. 185–186, and E. G. Huzar's *Mark Antony*, p. 182.)

CHAPTER 8:
The Warrior Queen

On the much-debated question as to whether Antony and Cleopatra were married see M. Grant's *Cleopatra* (pp. 185–187); he thinks they were not legally married (certainly they were not in Roman eyes) but united by a "sacred marriage" as were Caesar and Cleopatra—two divinities—Antony-Dionysus and Cleopatra-Isis. This was accepted in the East and gave legitimacy to their children.

CHAPTER 9:
The Battle of Actium

The Battle of Actium. Widely differing and confused reports of this strange battle have caused endless debate. It is now generally accepted by most scholars that Antony and Cleopatra's flight from the battle was a planned escape, despite Roman insistence that it was Cleopatra's cowardice and treachery and Antony's passion for the Queen that led to their defeat. Some think they were defeated before the battle began. (See J. M. Carter's *The Battle of Actium*, especially pp. 237–238, E. Bradford's *Cleopatra,* pp. 237–238, and M. Grant's *Cleopatra*, pp. 208–238.) R. Syme in his *Roman Revolution* thinks that Antony and Cleopatra were a pretext and used as pawns by Octavius to create the war to gain his supremacy over the Mediterranean world. See pp. 274–275 and 296–297.

CHAPTER 11:
Aftermath

As to **Cleopatra's reputation today,** her underlying glamor and her bold sex appeal are exemplified by Elizabeth Taylor's movie portrayal of the Queen. The one-sided image, omitting all other attributes, is the image this generation has been brought up on. (See L. Hughes-Hallett's *Cleopatra: Histories, Dreams and Distortions*, especially pp. 295–300—but the whole book is fascinating on the images of Cleopatra's character left by changing generations according to their own views on life and morals.)

BIBLIOGRAPHY

An asterisk indicates books of particular interest to young adult readers

Bean, George E. *Turkey: An Archeological Guide*. New Jersey: Plowman & Littlefield, 1971.

*Bradford, E. *Cleopatra*. London: Hodder & Stoughton, 1971.

Brooks, P., and Walworth, N. *When the World Was Rome*. New York: J. B. Lippincott, 1972.

Carter, J. M. *The Battle of Actium*. London: Hamish Hamilton, 1970.

Casson, L. *The Ancient Mariners*. New York: Funk & Wagnall's, 1959.

*_____ *Ancient Egypt*. New York: Time-Life Ages of Man series, 1965.

Cavafy, C. P. *Collected Poems*. Princeton, N. J.: Princeton University Press, 1975.

*Forster, E. M. *Alexandria: A History and Guide*. Woodstock, N. Y.: Overlook Press, 1974.

Bibliography

Fraser, Antonia. *The Warrior Queen.* New York: Knopf, 1989.

Grant, Michael. Cleopatra. London: Weidenfeld & Nicholson, 1972.

_____*From Alexander to Cleopatra.* New York: Charles Scribner's Sons, 1982.

Hughes-Hallett, Lucy. *Cleopatra: Histories, Dreams and Distortions.* New York: HarperCollins, 1990.

Huzar, Eleanor Goltz. *Mark Antony: A Biography.* Minneapolis: University of Minnesota Press, 1978.

*Lindsay, Jack. *Cleopatra.* New York: Coward, McCann & Geoghegan, 1971.

*Plutarch. *The Lives of Noble Grecians and Romans.* Encyclopedia Britannica, Inc. Chicago, 1955. Translation by J. Dryden, revised by A. H. Clough.

Rostovtzeff, Mikhail I. *Social and Economic History of the Hellenistic World.* London: Oxford University Press, 1941.

*Shakespeare, William. *Antony and Cleopatra.*

Suetonius, G. *The Lives of Twelve Caesars.* Translation by R. Graves. Penguin Books, 1957.

Syme, Ronald. *The Roman Revolution.* London: Oxford University Press, 1960.

Tarn, W. W. *Cambridge Ancient History,* Vol X. Cambridge: Cambridge University Press, 1924.

Volkmann, H. *Cleopatra: Politics and Propaganda.* (Trans. by T. J. Cadoux.) New York: Sagamore Press, 1958.

*Weigall, Arthur E. *The Life and Times of Cleopatra, Queen of Egypt: A Study in the Origin of the Roman Empire.* New York: Greenwood Press, Rev. Ed. 1968.

Witt, R. E. *Isis in the Greco-Roman World.* Ithaca, N. Y.: Cornell University Press, 1971.

INDEX

Page references in *italics* indicate illustrations.

Actium, Battle of, 105–13

Agrippa, 103, 107, 111

Alexander Helios, 76, 88, 96, 127

Alexander the Great, 3, 67, 96, 138–39
  and Julius Caesar, 54, 55
  and Parthia, 14, 96

Alexandria, 139
  description of, 3, 5–6, 9–11, 33–34, 36
  and Julius Caesar, 53
  victory celebration in, 93–97

animals
  attitudes toward, 6, 21
  in triumph parades, 49

Antony. *See* Mark Antony.

Antony and Cleopatra (Shakespeare), 72, 114

Aphrodite, 51
  Cleopatra as, 16, 68, 70
  Octavia as, 81

Arabic language, 9, 25

Armenia, 90, 91, 93, 96

Arsinoë, 38, 39, 42, 49, 71, 121

Artemesia, 66, 142

asp, Egyptian, *125*, 125–26

Athens, 81, 101

balsam plantations, 89

barges, royal and ceremonial, 19, 21, *22*, 42, 68, 70

Berenice, 14, 15

Brutus, 58, 64, 66, 67

bull, sacred, 20–21

Caesar. *See* Julius Caesar.

Caesar Augustus. *See* Octavius.

Caesarion
  as Cleopatra's heir, 61, 62, 63, 66, 71, 96
  death of, 127
  escape plan for, 115, 124
  and Julius Caesar, 43, 50, 63, 96

Caesarium (temple), 34

calendars, 33, 53

Calpurnia, 51

Cassius, 58, 64, 66, 67

Cato, 47, 48, 56

Cavafy, C.P., 93, 118

cedar trees, 86

Charmion, 119, 124

Cicero, 47, 48, 54, 64

Index

civil wars, Roman, 47, 64, 78,
103–4
Cleopatra, *10, 52, 104, 122*
as Aphrodite, 16, 68, 70, 93
in art and drama, 72, 129,
145
children of, 42, 43, 76, 85,
88, 89, 93, 95–96, 116
death of, 119–26, *122,* 129
and Dionysian rites, 73–74
Egyptian culture and, 16,
20–24
family and childhood of, 7,
9, 12, 13
Greek culture and, 2, 3, 4,
129
and Isis, 2, 9, 16, 20, 21,
42, 43, 44, 45, 51, 62, 68,
76, 93, 101, 124
and Julius Caesar, 31–43,
50–54, 60
and King Herod, 80, 86, 88,
89
and Mark Antony, 15,
66–76, 77, 85–89, 91,
93–98, 99–113, 114–20,
124, 128
marriages of, 16–17, 42
Nile River voyages of,
19–24, 42
and Octavius, 66, 103–4,
116, 121
political objectives of, 2, 11,
62, 86, 98, 115, 121, 128
political skills of, 1–2, 11,
14, 25, 43, 89, 100

propaganda against, 2, 66,
73–74, 92, 97, 99–100,
102–4, 128, 134
and Ptolemy XIII as rival,
18, 24–25, 29–33, 35–42
and relationship with Rome,
11, 24, 25, 53, 64, 66,
103–4, 128
in Rome, 50–60
royal barge of, 42, 68
showmanship of, 8–9, 17,
70, 93
as Venus, 51
as warrior queen, 99–104,
109–13
Cleopatra Selene, 76, 88, 96, 127
Cleopatra's Needles, 34
cobra (Egyptian asp), 17, *125,*
125–26
Crassus, 12, 14, 26, 90
Crete, 96
Cyndus (river), 68
Cyprus, 13, 33, 62
Cyrene, 96

dancing, and Dionysus, 7, 8,
73–74
date-palm plantations, 89
Dionysus, 140
festivals and rites of, 7, 8,
74, 93–97, 101
Mark Antony as, 67
Ptolemy XIII as, 16
divine titles, and rulers, 16, 52,
67, 70, 93–94
See also Dionysus; Isis; Osiris.

Index

"Donations of Alexander," 97, 144

Egypt. *See also* Alexandria.
  and Greek culture, 2–3
  independence of, 2, 13–14, 115, 121, 128
  overseas possessions of, 62, 86
  religion of, 20–24
  and Rome, 4, 12–15
  supplies and wealth of, 12, 105, 115
  taxation in, 3, 13, 15, 18, 62
Ephesus, 99, 100
Euphrates River, 81, 89, 90

festivals and ceremonies
  Dionysian, 7, 8, 73–74, 101
  Egyptian, 16–17, 20–24, 93–97, *94–95*
  Roman, 48–50
"Flute Player" (Ptolemy XII), 7–8, *8*
Fulvia, 64, 71, 76, 77, 78

games, and Roman triumphs, 49–50
Gaul, and Caesar, 14, 26, 48
Golden Age, dream of, 98
Greece
  and Battle of Actium, 105–13
  culture of, in Alexandria, 2–3, 5–6, 33, 34
  and Mark Antony, 75, 81, 101
gymnasium, in Alexandria, 6, 93

Hebrew language, 9, 25
Herod, King, 80, 81, 86, 88, 89, 116, 143
Horace, 99, 126

India, 54, 115
"Inimitable Livers," 72–73, 116
Iras, 119, 124
Isis, *44*, 67, 69, 87, 141
  Cleopatra as, 2, 16, 21, 42, 43, 68, 93, 101, 124
  qualities of, 9, 45

Jews, in Alexandria, 9
Jordan, 86
Judaea, 14, 62, 80, 81, 86, 88
Julian calendar, 53
Julius Caesar, *28*
  in Alexandria, 29–43
  assassination of, 56–57, *58–59*
  and Caesarion, 43, 63, 96
  as dictator, 46–60
  in Gaul, 14, 26
  and Parthia, 53–54
  personality and character of, 12, 30, 31–33, 57, 64
  as Pompey's rival, 26–29
  and Ptolemy XIII, 35–39
  reputation of, 57, 63
  victory parade of, 48–50
Jupiter, 49

languages, and Cleopatra, 9, 25, 90
Lebanon, 62, 86
Lepidus, 64, 67, 78

Index

library, in Alexandria, 6, 33
liquor, and Dionysian rites, 7, 74

Macedonia, 2, 96
makeup (cosmetics), *17, 18,* 80
Mark Antony, *65*
  as Alexander the Great, 67,
    76, 91
  at Battle of Actium, 105–13
  character and tastes of, 64,
    70–71, 72, 78, 91, 97,
    113, 114, 116
  and Cleopatra, 15, 62,
    66–76, 77, 85–89, 91,
    93–98, 99–113, 114–20,
    124, 128
  as Dionysus, 67, 68, 70, 81,
    93, 97, 117
  final days of, 116–20
  as Hercules, 15, 65
  and Julius Caesar, 50–51,
    54–55, 57
  and marriage to Octavia,
    79, 81, 82–84, 92, 101,
    102
  and Octavius, 64–67,
    77–84, 86, 92, 96, 97
  as Osiris, 93
  and Parthia, 71, 75, 85, 86,
    89–91, 95
  political governance of, 86,
    130
  popularity of, 63, 97, 100
  propaganda against, 92, 97,
    99–100, 102–4
marriage
  brother-sister, 16, 141

between divine rulers, 51,
    70, 102, 144
  Roman, and politics, 51, 78
medical research, in Alexan-
    dria, 33, 139

naval battle, at Actium, 105–13
Nile River, 3, 17, *40–41*
  annual flooding of, 18,
    61–62, 141–42
  and Cleopatra, 19–24
  and Isis, 20
  and Osiris, 17, 20
North Africa, 47, 48, 49

Octavia, 79, 81, 82–84, 88,
    92, 101, 102
Octavius
  as Caesar's heir, 63
  and Cleopatra, 66, 103–4,
    116, 121
  in Egypt, 115–24, 128
  history's view of, 129–30
  and Mark Antony, 64–67,
    77–84, 86, 92, 96, 97
  as politician, 92, 97,
    99–100, 102–4, 121
omens, 106, 117
oracles, 5, 54, 76, 97–98,
    139–40
Osiris, 17, 20, 93

palace, royal, in Alexandria,
    5–6, 29, 30
Palestine, 62
Parthia
  and Caesar, 53–54

and Crassus, 14, 26
and Mark Antony, 71, 75,
    81, 85, 86, 90–91, 95, 96
military tactics of, 90, 91
and Syria, 80
"Parthian shot," 90
"Partners in Death," 116
Pharos Lighthouse, 6, 34,
    36–37, 48, 139
Plutarch, 1, 138
Pompey, 12, 14–15, 26–29, 48,
    53, 81
Pothinus, 24, 30, 34, 38, 48
Proculius, 120
propaganda
    anti-Cleopatra, 2, 66,
        73–74, 128, 134
    against Antony and Cleopa-
        tra, 92, 97, 99–100,
        102–4
    Cleopatra's use of, 70
    and Sibylline Books, 54
Propertius, 105
Ptolemaic dynasty, 2–3, 4, 6–7
    and Egyptian culture, 23–4
    and intermarriage, 16
    and Rome, 11
Ptolemy Caesar. See Caesarion
Ptolemy Philadelphus, 89,
    96, 127
Ptolemy XII, 7–9, 8, 11–15
Ptolemy XIII
    guardians of, 24–25, 30, 34,
        38, 48
    as husband, 16
    as rival, 18, 24–25, 29–33,
        34–42

Ptolemy XIV, 42, 61

Re, 20–21
religion
    Eastern, 74
    Egyptian, 20–24
    Roman, 21–22, 51, 128
Roman Empire, 66–67, 130
Roman law
    and the army, 27
    and inheritance, 103
Roman Republic, 12, 47–48,
    66–67, 140–1
    Cleopatra's views of, 53
    and Julius Caesar, 27, 47
Roman senate, 12, 55, 56,
    58–59, 100
Roman women, and marriage,
    51, 78
Rome
    and Cleopatra, 2, 11, 24, 25,
        50–53, 64, 66, 102–4, 128
    military power of, 4, 50
    and Ptolemy XII, 11–15
    and religion, 21–22, 51,
        128
    territories of, 44 B.C., 59
    victory parades in, 48–50,
        120, 121

Samos (island), 101
"Sea King," 81–82, 106
Shakespeare, William, 72, 114
ships and shipbuilding, 38, 64,
    86, 115. See also barges,
    royal and ceremonial.
Sibylline Books, 54, 139

Index

Sibylline Oracles, 5, 54, 76,
    97–98, 139–140
solar calendar, 33, 53
Sosigenes (astronomer), 33, 50,
    53, 139
Syria, 14, 24, 25, 62, 76, 80,
    81, 86

Tarsus (town), 67, 68
taxation, in Egypt, 3, 13, 15,
    18, 62

triumphs (victory parades),
    48–50, 93–97, 120, 121
Triumvirate, first, 26
Triumvirate, second, 64,
    66–67, 78–79, 97

Venus, 51, 70
Virgil, 79, 88

zoological garden, in
    Alexandria, 6